Us

A Journalist's Look at the Culture, Conflict and Creativity of the South

Adam Parker

The Post and Courier
Charleston, South Carolina

Edited by Doug Pardue

EVENING POST
BOOKS
Our Accent is Southern!

Parker, Adam *Us: A Journalist's Look at the Culture, Conflict and Creativity of the South*

Published by Evening Post Books, Charleston, South Carolina.

ISBN-13: 978-1-929647-75-0

Cover design by Gil Shuler
Interior design by Michael J. Nolan

Adam Parker earned two degrees in music, then spent a decade in the business world before going back to school for a graduate degree in journalism from Columbia University. At *The Post and Courier*, he has worked on several beats over the years, including religion, the arts and, most recently, race and history. A long-time student of the civil rights movement and race in America, he has written extensively about the African-American experience. He is the author of the biography "Outside Agitator: The Civil Rights Struggle of Cleveland Sellers Jr.," published by Hub City Press in 2018, and "Us: A Journalist's Look at the Culture, Conflict, and Creativity of the South," published by Evening Post Books.

Photo by Mark Stetler

Contents

III. *PEOPLE: Confronting Life*

Introduction by Jennifer Berry Hawes

Vertamae: A Profile

Ambassadors of Gullah Culture: Ron and Natalie Daise keep up the storytelling

The Chill of Death: Korean War veteran recounts horrors of the Battle of Chosin

From Charleston to New York and Back Again: James Campbell's long reach

The Odyssey: From Liberia to the Lowcountry, mayhem to music-making

Nelson B. Rivers III: From protester to pastor

Pat Conroy Talks: Beloved S.C. author, turning 70, forced to endure celebration and praise

How Polly Sheppard, a Survivor of the Emanuel AME Church Mass Shooting, Carries On

IV. *THE ARTISTIC IMPULSE: Confronting Human Nature*

Introduction by Mark Sloan

The Quandary of Alice Ravenel Huger Smith

Confronting Nature and Time: Two McClellanville artists find their place

'One-Man Preservation Army': Ronald Ramsey captures memories of Charleston's changing cityscape

The Great Curator: Charles Wadsworth, beloved chamber music impresario, to retire

The Johnson Collection: How S.C.'s largest private art collection transformed an old mill town

Making Sense of It: After Charleston church shooting, artists help public digest the horror

Lost Homes: Charleston artist recalls destructive impact of roadway projects

Making Omar: The story of Spoleto Festival's opera about an enslaved Muslim scholar in the Carolinas

Acknowledgements

Foreword

by John L.S. Simpkins

In the short story, "Shooting an Elephant," George Orwell inhabits the form of a colonial functionary in Moulmein, Burma. He has been sent to maintain imperial order among a brown population described in the most dehumanizing terms, though they were in common usage during his time. In the semi-autobiographical tale, a British policeman butchers a valuable beast of burden, an elephant in "must," mainly to avoid appearing weak. Orwell depicts the revelation below:

> I perceived in this moment that when the white man turns tyrant it is his own freedom that he destroys. He becomes a sort of hollow, posing dummy, the conventionalized figure of a sahib. For it is the condition of his rule that he shall spend his life in trying to impress the "natives," so that in every crisis he has got to do what the "natives" expect of him. He wears a mask and his face grows to fit it.

Orwell's imperial police officer goes on to describe the burden he carried, saying his "whole life, every white man's life in the East, was one long struggle not to be laughed at."

There is much in Orwell's writing that reminds me of Adam Parker, but not in the way one might assume. Like Orwell, Adam has been a citizen of the world, not entirely anchored or rooted in one geography or collection of folkways. As with the former Eric Arthur Blair, Adam has chronicled his travels with a reportorial eye for detail and connection to broader themes and struggles.

But it is Orwell's character in "Shooting an Elephant" that most deeply resonates when it comes to describing a core element of Adam's writing. One of the qualities I admire most about Adam Parker, as a writer and as a friend, is that he roams this world largely free of Orwell's white man's burden. To be sure, he is a white man, but his awareness of that socially-constructed reality has not forced him into wearing the mask Orwell describes. Rather than centering himself in his stories, Adam seeks to both connect and understand, bringing others along in ways that, like a day-long light rain, can be slowly, quietly, and deeply revelatory.

In the stories that follow, the reader will encounter characters and ideas on their own terms. Each account places the reader in the story with narration intended to illuminate, rather than centering the storyteller. The result is a continual discovery of big ideas within small stories.

Freed of the need to be the "corpse at every funeral, the bride at every wedding and the baby at every christening," Adam can train his keen observational skills on the subject at hand. It's not about him. He has rejected the mask and the tyranny that accompanies it for an authentic critical curiosity of the fundamental elements of identity, culture and difference. We are the richer for it.

Adam's capacious appetite for experiencing the world and the people in it has found an appropriate home in Charleston, South Carolina. This multi-layered siren-city of my home state is one of the rare American locales that is both global and Southern at its core. Its promise and problems remain on display in plain sight through what occurs within its bounds and the connections that emanate therefrom. Charleston remains a powerful vantage point from which one can engage the South, the United States, and the world beyond. As setting, and sometimes as character, it has and will continue to reveal much of who we were, who we are, and who we can be.

Adam Parker's writing illuminates all of those areas of inquiry and brings us along for the ride. That is a burden worthy of bearing. Any fellow traveler will find this to be an enlightening journey.

I.

RACE AND HISTORY:
Confronting American Identity

Introduction

by the Rev. Joseph Darby

The saying "Those who cannot remember the past are condemned to repeat it" is generally attributed to writer and philosopher George Santayana. Adam Parker affirms that saying in this collection of his stories on Race and History over the last 15 years.

From his stories on remembering the Holocaust experience to his stories reflecting the trials and triumphs of Americans of African descent and America's ongoing racial conflict, Adam brings a distinct, clear and perceptive voice to how far America has come in terms of confronting race, culture and class and how far America still has to go.

Adam's stories led me to a moment of reflection and recollection as I read them. I was in my early teens during the civil rights movement of the 1960s and, like many of my peers, I badly wanted to get involved. My widowed mother, however, vetoed that possible action on my part. She made it plain that she was not about to let her only son be placed in harm's way.

I used to lament the fact that I wasn't able to be an active participant in the movement that led to the Civil Rights Act of 1964 and the Voting Rights Act of 1965 — laws that many thought ended the quest for freedom, justice and equity in the United States. The still-evolving fight for equity and justice in America has proved me wrong. Even in the present day, there's still work to be done and the battle goes on.

I celebrate Adam Parker's insight and his perceptive sensitively to the issues and concerns that still linger and trouble our nation in the current day and that are reflected in his writings on race and history.

Adam's writing reminds us that we still have miles to go. It also reminds us that people of conscience and good will have to walk together. I hope that his words inspire you to do so in the quest for "Liberty and justice for all." Do so in the spirit on my ancestors in the faith, who said, in spite of enslavement and segregation, "Walk together, children, don't you get weary. There's a great camp meeting in the promised land."

A Mother's Love

Slave sack contains passions of past, present

When it was first made, perhaps in 1840, it probably held rice, seeds, animal feed or cereal, but later it was filled with love.

The embroidered words start halfway down the front of the sack, words stitched in brown, red and green yarn, forming a beautifully rounded script that runs evenly across one side.

The words combine to tell a story, a story of love and loss, of generations, a story of past and present and future, a story at once personal and communal, for the individual tragedy it recounts is shared by thousands of others.

The Osnaburg cloth sack, 33 inches by 16 inches, was made of the same material used to make a slave's clothing, a coarse linen called "Negro cloth."

Stained and torn in places, someone long ago made an effort to repair the sack, applying patches to the worn areas, careful to keep the rough side of the patch on the inside.

This old sack, torn yet treasured — once by a young girl and again 150 years later by those who stand in awe of what once happened — this old sack, buried under meaningless doilies and scraps of cloth for sale at a flea market, has been reclaimed by history.

And this is the story it tells:

> *My great grandmother Rose*
> *mother of Ashley gave her this sack when*
> *she was sold at age 9 in South Carolina*
> *it held a tattered dress 3 handfulls of*
> *pecans a braid of Roses hair. Told her*
> *It be filled with my LOVE always*
> *she never saw her again*
> *Ashley is my grandmother*
>
> *Ruth Middleton*
> *1921*

Pam Lane found the sack at an open-air flea market in Springfield, Tenn., 45 miles northeast of Nashville, where she lives with her husband and three children.

Lane said she was picking through a collection of crocheted doilies and miscellaneous embroidered items on a Saturday afternoon in February when she came upon the slave sack.

"I had the sack in my hand but didn't notice it at first," she said. "I could read part of it."

She quickly realized she had stumbled upon a precious object.

"I figured it was worth a ton of money!"

She offered the seller $20 for a small bundle of cloth, including the sack, returned home and sat down at the computer. She Googled "Middleton" and "slave" and other keywords in an attempt to shed light on her discovery. Again and again, the search results returned "Middleton Place Plantation."

After a few days, she decided to call.

Tracey Todd, vice president of museums at Middleton Place, answered that call. A homemaker from Nashville told him about an old sack she had found.

"I got goose bumps, chills. I immediately realized that what she had could be something special," he said.

Lane and Todd exchanged several e-mails and phone calls over the next several days. The Nashville mother was thinking of auctioning the sack on eBay. It's part of an established routine: She buys items at flea markets and rummage sales, then sells the stuff online to raise enough money for her 9-year-old daughter's private school tuition.

Todd asked her to hold off. She would have to take a photograph of the sack for eBay anyway; why not send him the picture so he could understand better the nature of the object in question? She did.

She also called Skinner auction house in Massachusetts, and an appraiser there said he'd research this unusual find and get back to her.

Lane spoke with Barbara Doyle, Middleton's historian. Doyle said Rose and Ruth were very common slave names, but the name Ashley was odd. In the 19th century, it usually applied to white males, not slave girls. But maybe it was acquired later. Or maybe it was a nickname, referring to the Ashley River.

Records show many Roses and Ruths at various Middleton family plantations in South Carolina, especially the plantations along the Combahee River, which spills into St. Helena Sound.

There was a Rose at Middleton Place in the 1860s. Middleton historians are poring over records, hoping to learn more about this family.

Todd told Lane about his efforts to examine the legacy of slavery in South Carolina and the interpretive programs of the Middleton Place Foundation. But at a certain point during the conversation, the subject shifted from the professional to the personal. Both are parents.

"We started talking about our children," Todd said. Together they tried to imagine what it might have been like to say goodbye forever.

Lane kept digging for information.

"I'd get on my computer and my eyes would swell all up."

Then she had a dream, a fuzzy dream about a sack and a little girl and a fistful of pecans ...

Next morning, Lane sent Todd a note: Make me an offer, even if it's just $1, and the sack is yours.

She got $100 and a lifetime membership to Middleton Place.

A little later, the appraiser from Skinner called back. He had never before encountered such an item, but figured it was worth $1,500 to $2,000. It likely could fetch much more than that at auction, he said.

But Lane didn't regret her decision for a second. She was glad the sack was in the hands of people who really care about it and are working to make it part of the grand, tragic sweep of American history.

"I've never had anything in my possession that I feel so strongly about," she said. "Stop and think: This is only three generations away."

A daughter sold. Torn from her mother: a mother who loved her, a mother who had nothing to give but love.

A sackful of love. Always.

May 24, 2008

Voyage to Freedom

Inspired by Amistad revolt, church sets course toward racial equality

This story ends with a celebration of culture, accomplishment and art. It begins with a mutiny.

In Charleston Harbor floats a tall ship called the Amistad. The name is Spanish for "friendship." It's a reproduction of the original black schooner once used for coastal transport, bringing captive Africans from the Caribbean to the United States.

The ship is in town to remind us of our country's terrible adolescence and its commitment to freedom and justice, to mark the bicentennial of the abolition of the trans-Atlantic slave trade, to draw attention to a contemporary opera produced by Spoleto Festival USA and to provide an added reason to stroll the waterfront and contemplate the horizons of history.

Circular Congregational Church and Plymouth Congregational Church presented a special Amistad service at Circular Congregational Church on May 17. Nichole Green, curator/director of the Old Slave Mart Museum, addressed the gathering. So did Lucille Whipper, the nearly 80-year-old former state legislator and activist. Representatives from the national United Church of Christ organization, Amistad America Inc., which owns and operates the schooner, and members of the ship's crew also attended.

In 2000, the United Church of Christ built a 4,800-square-foot Amistad Chapel at its national headquarters in Cleveland.

In 1999, the Amistad reproduction was dedicated in a Connecticut ceremony. The project to re-create the "low, black schooner" was funded in large part by the United Church of Christ.

In 1957, the United Church of Christ was formed after Congregationalists joined with Reformed and Evangelical Christians. Long before this merger, though, there was Jim Crow, and slavery before that — injustices that many Congregationalists of the 19th century opposed on religious grounds.

These abolitionists included Lewis and Arthur Tappan, brothers who descended from Benjamin Franklin and became successful merchants and philanthropists in New York City, and James W.C. Pennington, an escaped slave who became a linguist, orator and writer.

During the 1830s, these three men actively condemned slavery. The Tappan brothers received death threats. Their businesses were boycotted, their property set aflame. On one occasion, Lewis Tappan received a package in which sat the amputated ear of a slave.

Their accomplishments, and the impact of the institutions they helped found, are recounted in the book "On the Heels of Freedom" by Joyce Hollyday.

When, in 1839, the Amistad was discovered off the Connecticut coast, and its rebellious black cargo was carted off to jail in New Haven to await trial for murder, mutiny and piracy, Lewis Tappan saw the best opportunity yet to put his abolitionist words into action.

On Sept. 3, Tappan joined forces with Joshua Leavitt and Simeon Jocelyn to form the Amistad Committee, entrusted with raising money to pay for the mutineers' legal defense. On March 9, 1841, the U.S. Supreme Court set the captives free, ruling that they had been illegally kidnapped and were entitled to return to Africa.

Pennington, a strong advocate for the imprisoned black mutineers, rejoiced at their release and assembled black colleagues from five states to host some of the Amistad Africans and find a way to help them get home.

Pennington formed the Union Missionary Society, which later would merge with the Amistad Committee to become the American Missionary Association.

Pushing for 'normal'

In a telephone interview, Hollyday said she wrote her book about the American Missionary Association because "it's a very rich story and one that was about to be lost."

The main goals of the association were to put an end to slavery, to establish schools to teach blacks (and train teachers who, in turn, could further the education of former slaves and their descendants), and to advance racial equality and Christian values.

To do that, the organization founded hundreds of primary and secondary schools and colleges throughout the South, some of which survive today in different forms.

Atlanta University, Fisk University and Howard University were formed with association support. Tougaloo College and Talladega College, too. And the Avery Normal Institute here in Charleston.

"In 1863, as soon as the ink was dry on the Emancipation Proclamation, the American Missionary Association put out a call for missionary teachers, in an effort to reach as many of the 4 million newly freed citizens as possible," wrote Hollyday.

It was courageous work, she said. Many of these teachers, white and female, came from the north and were harassed or worse. Black students, hungry for education, walked for miles to get to the newly established schools, set up in a barn or church or open field, Hollyday said. If they had no money, they would pay tuition with chickens. The purpose was to train local residents to further the goals of the educational mission, to empower Southern blacks to take control of their destiny, Hollyday said.

Some of these early schools developed into "normal" schools, institutions that focused on the humanities and trained their students to be teachers. Some served as meeting places, eventually providing leaders of the civil rights movement a safe haven in which to plan their campaigns.

The Dorchester Academy in Birmingham, Ala., educated young black children until 1940 when it was converted into the Dorchester Center, a facility soon to be used by Andrew Young and Martin Luther King Jr.

In the 1940s and 1950s, as public schools opened their doors to black students, many of these American Missionary Association schools closed. Others became part of the new state-run system. This was a mixed blessing, Hollyday said, for while it signified that progress was being made, it also institutionalized the "separate but equal" doctrine that led to inferior treatment of black students.

The association's old schools, which had served blacks so well for so long, were on the wane, "so there was a great sense of loss," Hollyday said.

A contribution

Lucille Whipper was a student at the Avery Normal Institute in the early 1940s when it was an association high school. She went on to study at Talladega College in Alabama, another American Missionary Association institution, now home to Hale Woodruff's famous mural of the Amistad revolt.

Whipper said her 1944 graduating class from Avery was the first to apply en masse to the College of Charleston, challenging its whites-only policy. But it didn't work, she said. The school became private a few years later to avoid the contentious issue of desegregation. (Its first black students enrolled in 1967.)

Whipper remembers the annual visits to Talladega by the association's executive secretary. While there, she joined a student group that fought to integrate Alabama's colleges and universities.

In 1947, Avery became a public school. In 1954, the same year the U.S. Supreme Court determined that "separate educational facilities are inherently unequal" in the landmark Brown v. Board of Education case, the Charleston County School Board closed Avery, citing financial problems.

In the mid-1970s, Whipper went to work at the College of Charleston as assistant to the president. She and other Avery graduates wanted to preserve the dilapidated and vacant building and the heritage it represented.

Whipper took charge, and in 1978, the Avery Institute of Afro-American History and Culture was established. When the institution, renamed the Avery Research Center, became part of the College of Charleston, Whipper served as its first president.

"From nothing came something," she said.

First to fight

The abolitionists of the 19th century, exercising their pious resolve, were not afraid to reach out to blacks, to offer aid, to defend them in court. The story of the Amistad mutiny captivated them and gave them new reason to fight for the rights of captured Africans and American slaves.

In their way, they fought as hard, and for much longer, than the ship's mutineers. But it started with 49 men and four children from the Mendi region of Africa, rice farmers, leopard hunters and blacksmiths. These were the survivors of the terrible Middle Passage that took them from Africa to Havana, "two and two chained together by hand and foot night and day," according to an Amistad trial deposition.

In Cuba, Jose Ruiz bought the men for $450 each. Pedro Montes bought the boy and three girls. The Amistad was prepared for its journey up the coast.

Misbehavior, such as drinking the crew's water, resulted in severe beatings, Hollyday writes in "On the Heels of Freedom." Then the wounds were rubbed with salt, gunpowder and rum.

"On the third night of the voyage, when a fierce thunderstorm covered the noise and distracted the crew, Sengbe (a captive) used (a) nail to pick the locks on the neck irons," Hollyday writes. The Africans found large knives and attacked the crew, the next day ordering them to sail east, back across the ocean. But by night Montes directed the ship northwest instead, hoping to encounter another ship and be rescued.

The ship foundered at sea for two months before the crew of the Washington found it off the East Coast and towed it to shore in New London, Conn. And then the trials began.

Freedom singing

A century and a half later, the American Missionary Association has become part of the United Church of Christ's Justice and Witness Ministries, focusing on social and economic justice, health and welfare and community empowerment. And the low, black schooner has come back to life, and with it a compelling history of sacrifice, moral fortitude and change. The Amistad trials, and John Quincy Adams' forceful argument before the Supreme Court — that these entrapped Africans were free because they were free all along — gave impetus to a new era.

After two centuries of slavery, the promised land was finally visible in the distance, emerging from the mist that had obscured it for so long.

The Redneck Shop and the Preacher

In Laurens, a long saga of racial conflict continues

LAURENS — The Rev. David Kennedy is not sure what he will do with the old theater building that his church has owned since 1997, but at least now he can start to think about it.

Maybe it will become a small museum that presents the horrors of slavery and Jim Crow. Maybe it will become a shared event space. Maybe the perfectly named New Beginning Missionary Baptist Church, which has moved — not always by choice — several times over the years will make a new beginning in the old Echo Theater.

For now, the property, located in the town's commercial center, is dust-filled and dilapidated, with only a few reminders of what went on there for nearly two decades. A small Confederate flag sticker remains affixed to the marquee. The name of the store that once occupied the building can be discerned through the sweeping scratch marks on the glass door.

The Redneck Shop once sold Confederate merchandise. In a twist of fate, the deed to the building was transferred to New Beginning Church in 1997, but its black congregation and activist preacher could do nothing so long as the store proprietor, John Howard, remained alive.

A legal stipulation in the deed had created a "life estate" that protected Howard, who continued to run the shop rent-free despite the change of landlord.

Howard died on Sept. 6 at age 71, bringing the Redneck Shop saga to an end and inviting Kennedy and his supporters in Laurens to imagine a new story for their small community that has struggled with racism and misunderstanding.

The confrontations between Kennedy and Howard — the threats, the name-calling, the protests — have stopped, but many say racial discord persists in Laurens, and Kennedy's efforts to bring it to light continue to meet resistance.

Refusing the mask

Howard, a member of the Ku Klux Klan, was a white supremacist who resented Kennedy's protests and continued to operate the Redneck Shop until 2012, even though bad health kept him from having regular hours.

The store displayed Confederate flags, Klan robes and hoods, clothing imprinted with the Stars and Bars and other memorabilia of the Lost Cause. Howard hosted Klan and neo-Nazi gatherings in a back room. Through the turn of the 21st century, this former mill town continued to display the relics of Jim Crow and nurture racially charged sentiments, according to residents black and white.

Still today a monument stands in front of the courthouse "in memory of the boys in gray," erected "by the citizens of Laurens" in 1910, just three years before Kennedy's great uncle Richard Puckett was lynched at a railroad truss on Aug. 11, 1913. The frayed rope used to kill Puckett hung from a steel beam until 1985.

In all, 185 black men were lynched in South Carolina from 1877 (the end of Reconstruction) to 1950, according to the Equal Justice Initiative. Eleven were killed in Laurens County. So it's understandable that blacks in town objected to the Redneck Shop when it opened in the 1990s.

Kennedy, accustomed to public protest over racial issues since he was a child, has organized anti-drug marches, challenged restaurant owners and police officers over race-related issues, defended victims of injustice, burned Confederate flags and used his bullhorn to denounce those he considers racist.

He remembers when he was child and a group of white boys taunted him by flashing their naked front sides from a bluff near the projects where he grew up. He called for his grandfather, Albert Garlington, a large, tough man he admired and respected, a man who never hesitated to administer discipline and teach important life lessons. The young Kennedy assumed his grandfather would put those boys in their place.

Instead, Garlington stood there, glaring at them, then told them in measured tones to go on home. His grandson was dumbfounded and confused. Kennedy could not fully appreciate the dangers of being black in Jim Crow America.

"I was so disappointed," he said. "Why was my grandfather, a strong man, afraid? I hated thinking of him like that."

Kennedy decided early in his life to reject such deference, to refuse meek assent to the rules of segregation and white power.

"I don't wear a mask," he said.

Something positive

In 1997, things came to a head at the Redneck Shop, precipitated by the transfer of a deed.

Howard in 1994 had gifted the deed to the Echo Theater to a young protégé, Michael Eugene Burden. Things went south between the two men after Burden met and married Judy Burden a couple years later. She was part Native American and uncomfortable with the Klan, she said. She encouraged Burden to choose. "It's either that or me," she told him.

Angered, Howard evicted Burden and his new family from the basement apartment they used. Burden turned to Kennedy, his foe, for help, and he sold the deed in April 1997 to the black preacher for $1,000. In a deposition from a 2009 lawsuit challenging Howard's attempt to transfer the deed a second time, Burden said he didn't remember the details of the first transfer, saying he was likely under the influence of drugs or alcohol. But a judge determined the initial transaction was proper and binding.

The deed came with an important stipulation: Howard would be permitted to operate the shop, rent-free, until the day he died. New Beginnings Missionary Baptist Church now was landlord of the Redneck Shop but could do nothing other than organize protests.

The ruckus in the town's central square troubled some merchants. The protests were disruptive. On one occasion, SLED officers positioned themselves on the second floor of a nearby shop, where they had a clear sight line to the theater building.

Some in town thought that ignoring the Redneck Shop was the best strategy, according to Sharon Barnes, owner of Picture This Frame & Art, located around the corner. She visited the Confederate memorabilia store once and found it museum-like. It was Kennedy who blew things out of proportion, she and others said.

Debbie Campbell, owner of the Capitol Theatre and Cafe, said race relations have improved in Laurens.

"Blacks and whites are mixing more these days than ever before," Campbell said. Conflict arises only when Kennedy and other protesters make race an issue. Still, she's relieved that the Redneck Shop is defunct.

"No town needs something like that," she said.

Jonathan Irick, executive director of the Main Street Laurens USA merchant association, said it was easy for some merchants to pay little attention to the Redneck Shop because of its position just off the square. Few raised objections, he said.

Now that the property is available for redevelopment, Irick hopes it can be turned into something that benefits the community.

"There would be a strong interest locally to get something positive in there," he said.

Fear takes hold

During their year together free from the Klan, the Burdens attended New Beginnings Missionary Baptist Church and sought comfort among its members. Michael Burden, who according to legal documents had secured the deed to the Echo Theater building thanks to "a mutual friendship thing," told his wife about the sense of obligation he felt toward his mentor. Burden could not be reached for comment.

In August 1998, Burden was arrested on larceny charges and sentenced to prison that February. He spent nine years at the minimum-security Northside Correctional Institution in Spartanburg. After his release, Howard took him in, Judy Burden said, and soon after that he filed for divorce.

Today, Michael Burden is a truck driver in Texas, and Hollywood will soon release a feature film about the Redneck Shop saga called "Burden," written and directed by Andrew Heckler and starring Forest Whitaker, Usher, Tom Wilkinson, Tess Harper and Garrett Hedlund.

Judy Burden and Kennedy remain friends.

"He's a really wonderful man," she said. "You couldn't ask for a better person."

Her opinion of Kennedy has not endeared her to other whites in town.

"It's really been rough," she said. "I've had people spit on me, call me a n-word lover. It's been unreal. Some people you'd think were your friends, but when they find out, turn into a different person."

She said her neighbors misunderstand Kennedy. "He's just trying to change things for the better."

But that's not the view of many whites in Laurens. His aggressive activism rubs people the wrong way. He has been vocal about all kinds of issues. When his church was on Main Street, its windows were broken by vandals, Kennedy found Confederate stickers on the door and sometimes encountered dead snakes, cats or rats that had been tossed inside.

On Aug. 14, 2012, when he operated out of a makeshift church on S.C. Highway 127, the building burned to the ground. The fire started in an exhaust fan and an investigation revealed no criminal intent, but some of the town's African Americans remained suspicious. In any case, fear once again took hold among black worshipers, and fewer showed up to Kennedy's Sunday morning services, he said.

For and against

Recently, Kennedy backed Laurens County School District 55 Superintendent Stephen G. Peters, who is black, and threw his support behind a bond referendum that would have raised up to $109 million and resulted in a new high school. School officials said the school was needed to relieve overcrowding and to modernize classrooms.

The proposed bond issue would have increased property taxes in the county about $450 a year for homeowners under 65 with property whose fair market value is $200,000. It met with instant opposition among most whites while most blacks supported the measure, according to Kennedy and Peters.

Dianne Belsom, founder and president of the Laurens County Tea Party, led the "Vote No" campaign. She said the concern among opponents was purely financial. Median annual income per household in Laurens County is just $38,000, she said. Residents did not want to pay higher taxes.

"This was not about race for anybody," Belsom said, referring to Kennedy's protests. "Personally, I feel like they were desperate to get it passed, and they made it a racial issue to galvanize the black vote."

When she attended a NAACP meeting and heard Kennedy speak of Laurens' racist history and lack of progress, Belsom bristled, she said.

"I thought it was bull crap. Instead of celebrating the gains we've made, he's just a race-baiter stuck in the past. ... I feel like it was despicable that (the referendum) was made into a racial issue, and leaders on the other side did nothing to squelch that. Things would have simmered down."

Belsom has lived in Laurens for 17 years and always felt that people got along, she said.

"I'm sure there are people out there who are racist, on both sides. ...That's always going to exist to a small degree," she said.

But she disdains public displays of bigotry.

"I refused to patronize the Redneck Shop," Belsom said. "I used to boycott that place, I used to pray for that place to close. I want there to be racial harmony. I'm actually really brokenhearted."

Wrestling the pig

The referendum initiative prompted much more than taxpayer push-back. State Rep. Mike Pitts called for an investigation of the school district and of Peters, questioning whether school officials had bought votes.

"The race card is the final play of liberals when they know they are losing," Pitts wrote on Twitter. "Before this is over Dr. Stephen Peters will have racially divided this school district just as Barack Obama divided our nation."

Other social media posts referred to Peters disparagingly. A newspaper ad was published calling for Peters' resignation, noting that ACT scores had slipped the year before Peters assumed his post.

Barnes, owner of Picture This, offered four signed prints of Robert E. Lee, Stonewall Jackson, Nathan Bedford Forrest and J.E.B. Stuart, double matted with foam core backing, ready to be framed, "to the first person who comes by my shop ... with signatures of 100 people who's (sic) residence is in Laurens District 55, stating that they will vote NO on Sept. 5." The prize was worth $75.

Meanwhile, Kennedy protested with his bullhorn outside Belsom's home, and "Vote Yes" campaigners offered free fish dinners to people who could prove they cast a ballot. It got ugly.

Peters tried to remain calm in the midst of the storm, but he felt unsafe in Laurens, he said. Public criticism was one thing, but name-calling and intimidation was unacceptable.

"Some here could have stopped it, but didn't," Peters said. "It's like wrestling with a pig: you both get muddy, but the pig loves it."

The proposed bond issue was defeated on Sept. 5, with 77 percent voting "no." Voter turnout was about 37 percent. The Sept. 25 school board meeting became so contentious that law enforcement officers had to intervene. During the meeting, it was announced that Peters was taking an indefinite leave of absence for family reasons, effective immediately.

In conversation

Peters and Kennedy both are outspoken, even forceful in their rhetoric. They are wholly dedicated to addressing social inequity, each in his own way, and both provoke heated resistance from whites.

Kennedy's church now is located in Clinton, a few miles east of Laurens. The building is a former gun shop and shooting range, but thanks to renovation work has the smell of the new. A restaurant operates on the property. About 50 people join Kennedy for worship on Sundays.

Years ago, Charleston attorney Susan Dunn met Kennedy through Carolina Alliance for Fair Employment when they were working on labor issues. They became friends. Kennedy asked Dunn to fill in for him one Sunday several years ago because he needed to be at a protest in front of the Redneck Shop. She obliged.

Dunn said the preacher-activist is dedicated to the Laurens community, both blacks and whites. "His heart is in that place," Dunn said. "I think he sees his calling as a kind of prophet, and the job of a prophet is not to make people feel good, it's to speak truth to power."

So when black residents complain about racism, she said, whites should listen.

"People often just don't get the fact that when there is a power difference between two sides, when one side is scared of the other, and that side dismisses such concerns, it's a refusal to be in conversation, a rejection of one's neighbors," Dunn said.

Kennedy can't guarantee that racism in and around Laurens will end, but he can promise he won't run from it. And now that he's in full control of the Echo Theater, he can promise something else:

"I can say there will be no more racist ideas or business taking place in that building."

March 3, 2019

Why Segregated Institutions and Social Clubs Persist

Sometimes it's nice to get together with like-minded people, to enjoy the solidarity of a particular group. But what happens when that group is all-white, or all-black?

The recent controversy at the Charleston Rifle Club, which rejected its first black candidate for membership despite support he received from some white members, has drawn attention to the presence and purpose of such groups. Private organizations, such as the Rifle Club, are not subject to the anti-discrimination laws set forth in the Civil Rights Act of 1964. Indeed, to qualify legally as "private," an organization is obligated to make a selection when determining its membership, excluding some who apply. Making that selection come with certain benefits and certain risks.

The legacy of slavery and segregation continues to play out today, partly in the form of white or black social clubs as well as intentionally black organizations such as fraternities and sororities, colleges and universities, churches, burial societies and more. These black organizations were formed out of necessity and remain relevant because of persistent prejudice and discrimination, according to sources interviewed for this article.

As Charleston and other communities grapple with race-related issues, heightened in recent years by the 2015 shooting at Emanuel AME Church, the 2017 "Unite the Right" rally in Charlottesville, Va., the Black Lives Matter movement and national anthem protests, some are questioning the relevance of organizations that forbid membership to whole groups of people based on gender or race.

The purpose of private clubs

Men like to gather together, including the elites of Europe and the United States. They did so in an organized way in 17th century London when coffee and chocolate were all the rage and those who could afford to buy these imported foods gathered in cafes and enjoyed a camaraderie very much defined by class.

By the 19th century, private men's clubs were popping up left and right, especially in the United States, and the phenomenon wasn't limited to a particular geographical area. New York City saw an upwelling of establishments such as the Union Club, Yale Club and Metropolitan Club.

But in the South, where class and race were inextricably intertwined, urban elites formed all-white social clubs and other institutions designed to preserve and invigorate a social order in which whites were in charge and blacks were forced to keep to themselves.

A few of these groups had quasi-military origins: Whites concerned about slave revolts and, later, Yankee aggression formed militias and fraternized in what were called rifle clubs.

Membership in some of these private organizations lent prestige to privileged white men who often held important civic positions. Within these curtained buildings they could safely discuss all sorts of topics, gamble, play cards or break bread together.

In the South, these clubs — such as the Charleston Rifle Club, Hibernian Society and Carolina Yacht Club — were part of the superstructure of a segregated society, according to Kathryn Silva, a history professor at Claflin University. They reinforced a status quo that designated African Americans second-class citizens (or denied them the benefits of citizenship altogether).

This history continues to influence society today.

'In good fellowship'

During the long period of institutionalized slavery, black people learned to rely on themselves, said Kathryn Silva, a history professor at Claflin University. Some freed blacks migrated to the urban centers, formed black institutions and joined an emerging black professional class that included pastors, funeral home directors, educators and business entrepreneurs.

The result was a society within a society, in which black people functioned with a large degree of autonomy and limited interaction with whites. This social structure was the outcome of white rules and practices, not the explicit choice of African Americans. During Reconstruction, when black Americans were empowered, they often reached across racial lines to implement policies, such as public education, that benefited all people. But that period was short-lived. Soon whites asserted their power to disenfranchise blacks.

Urban African Americans once again were forced to rely on themselves and their communities, reinforcing key social pillars, such as church, home and school, according to the Rev. Joseph Darby, an AME Church leader in South Carolina. As Jim Crow segregation became the new norm, African Americans established and strengthened their institutions. Churches became places not just for worship but for social gatherings and political organization. School teachers strived to train a new generation of literate youth. A system of apprenticeship in the trades helped create a workforce that generated modest wealth.

Black people could not join private white social clubs, so they formed their own. In 1914, a group of 16 African-American men started the Charleston Owl's Whist Club so they might have a safe retreat for games of cards and socializing. Now 104 years old, the club has about 50 members, including State Rep. David Mack, State Sen. Marlon Kimpson, city Councilman Hillery Douglas, lawyer Anthony O'Neill, doctor Melvin Brown, club president Lecklyer Gaillard and club historian Willi Glee. They convene for monthly meetings and occasionally gather just for fun at the club's West Ashley property.

The club might be viewed as anachronistic, but it still serves a purpose since racism and discrimination continue to impact blacks, who consequently continue to seek "safe spaces," Silva said.

"A culture of racism has very much excluded black individuals," she said. "African-American organizations offer an alternative."

For Mack, the club offers a friendly space where busy people can find a respite from their daily toil.

"It's an opportunity for men to come together in good fellowship," he said. "That's what it's all about."

He said he doesn't care what other private clubs do, or who they exclude, so long as they don't benefit from direct or indirect public funding. But when people gather in good faith and with a generous spirit, they derive benefits that extend beyond the walls of the club.

"When people are in an environment like that, where they love each other and respect each other, when they move out into the world they tend to do the same thing," Mack said.

The Rev. Jeremy Rutledge, pastor of Circular Congregational Church and a leader in the Charleston Area Justice Ministry, said that safe black spaces are needed given the long history of racism in America.

"The thing that I hear most strongly is this idea that black cultural institutions really matter," he said. "The preservation of black cultural spaces, the church, the HBCUs, the neighborhood, the barbershop — when you've been oppressed for so long you need these black spaces. Those are survival spaces, those are resilient spaces."

They are essential for the preservation and celebration of black culture.

"White culture doesn't have a need to be preserved here, it's been so dominant," Rutledge said.

So some degree of cultural separation is to be expected.

"We are not trying to get everyone to go to the same church," he said. "What we want to do is create this community where were are welcomed into each other's cultural spaces, and where we learn from each other."

The ethic of African Americans, therefore, is not one of domination and control, but of freedom and resilience and struggle, he said.

The ethic (if one can call it that) of all-white groups like the Rifle Club, "is rooted in subjugation and oppression and who you want to keep out and how you want to control things," Rutledge said. "The context is very different."

'Advocates for change'

No white person has ever expressed an interest in joining the Owl's Whist Club, probably due to a reluctance to invade African American's "safe space." That's not the case at black churches and colleges.

About 10 percent of the student body and 28 percent of the faculty at Claflin is non-African-American. At S.C. State University, the only publicly funded HBCU in South Carolina, the non-African-American student population is about 4 percent and the non-African-American faculty population is about 16 percent.

All historically black colleges and universities in the U.S., public and private, though designed to provide black students with a safe space where they can explore their cultural identity, have some non-black students, and all proclaim an explicit commitment to diversity, Silva noted.

"HBCUs are not exclusively black," she said. "They were created as space for African Americans to go to school, but now are integrated, sometimes more so than white colleges."

"The percentage of HBCU students who were either white, Hispanic, Asian or Pacific Islander, or Native American was 17 percent in 2015, up from 13 percent in 1980," according to a Pew Research Center report published early last year. "Hispanic students, in particular, have seen their overall shares grow on HBCU campuses, increasing from 1.6 percent in 1980 to 4.6 percent in 2015."

For comparison, the College of Charleston is about 80 percent white; African Americans comprise about 8 percent of student enrollment. The University of South Carolina is about 77 percent white and 10 percent black.

Silva said most African Americans seek social reform. They want more equality and less discrimination. Many whites do too; but some seek to preserve the status quo.

"African Americans, as a group, see themselves as advocates for change," Silva said. "The way to deal with it is to be open."

But change can occur only if the rule-makers agree (or are overthrown). This places much of the burden for reform on whites, according to Rutledge. African Americans can protest injustice, confront wrongdoing and call for change, but if those in power resist such calls, society is left in a stalemate — just like the Rifle Club today.

"With historically black spaces, whites don't need much say in that," Rutledge said. "(It's) for the black community to decide (how they function). But the white community has an enormous responsibility in terms of everything else: private clubs, government agencies, religious and political institutions, what we teach in school. People with a disproportionate share of power have a disproportionate share of responsibility, particularly knowing how we got here."

'A prophetic voice'

The black church, which was institutionalized after the Civil War when whites ejected black worshipers from their sanctuaries, has played a central role in the lives of many African Americans, especially in the South. As one of the major pillars of black society, the church has served multiple purposes, religious and secular, spiritual and political. Church buildings often are used as meeting places. Much of the direct-action phase of the civil rights movement was designed in the basement of a church.

As a consequence, the church is inseparable from black identity and struggle, according to the Rev. Kylon Middleton, pastor of Mt. Zion AME Church. It was (and remains) a place where African Americans gain experience in leadership, organizational skills, public speaking, financial management and more.

"There was no leadership opportunity in secular realms, the playing field was not level to the extent that (black people) were able to be supervisors or in charge of anything," Middleton said.

So the church became a mechanism for leadership development, empowering its members, some of whom joined the board, led the choir, taught Sunday school, planned events, raised funds and so on, he said. The church trained generations of black people who had no such opportunities in a society controlled by whites.

"The black church also becomes a vehicle for wealth management and social uplift," he said. Members with more means often would help create a safety net that protected poor members.

In church, black people also learned public speaking skills and how to represent their community.

"Speeches and recitations were required of every young person ... who developed the poise necessary in order to captivate and keep people's attentions," Middleton said. "The expectation was that you will leave here knowing how to carry yourself, how to present yourself and represent the church. It was a source of identity."

And the church fostered social activism.

"In the black church you learn how to become a prophetic voice," Middleton said. "Ministers and leaders (were) wired for social justice." Churches in Charleston and other communities came together often, and any strike or protest invariably would be led, at least in part, by pastors.

Church members also were involved in the NAACP, founded by blacks and whites in 1909 at the height of the lynching crisis, and in black fraternities, schools, neighborhood groups and more.

"These things were all inextricably linked: the church, the civic groups and the cause," Middleton said. "This still happens. We look out for each other."

Under Scrutiny, Historic Lowcountry Plantations Consider Their Role in Dialogue on Race

Cairy Lester, a 55-year-old African American resident of Charlotte, has a cousin who won't step foot on a historic plantation site.

"No way," his cousin says. "Never." It doesn't matter how well the management team incorporates the terrible history of slavery; her aversion runs too deep.

Lester's cousin is far from alone. But Lester himself has visited several of Charleston's antebellum plantation sites, and his experiences have provoked mixed feelings, he said.

Recently, he was sitting on his couch late one evening thinking about Middleton Place and its beauty. It bothered him that people could get married there — at a place where Black people suffered and died in bondage.

"If it's not appropriate to have a wedding at a former Nazi concentration camp, it's really not appropriate to have a wedding at a plantation," he said. "There's a lot of pain associated with this place."

So Lester wrote a note to Middleton Place staffers expressing his concerns. What he wanted was, in a word, transparency, he said.

The next day, Jeff Neale, director of preservation and interpretation, called Lester — not to defend or justify Middleton Place's programming, but to listen.

"I have to admit I was impressed," Lester said. "I really shared my thoughts. ... He said, 'Why don't you come down to our Juneteenth program?' My wife and I went."

Neale also sent a link to the historic site's documentary called "Beyond the Fields: Slavery at Middleton Place," released in 2017.

It turned out that Middleton Place would cancel its Juneteenth program, at which several public figures had been scheduled to recite the names of around 3,000 enslaved people. The staff had received too many threats and, concerned for the safety of patrons and colleagues, felt compelled to shut it all down.

Drayton Hall, another historic plantation site along Ashley River Road, also has been receiving threats and recently boosted its onsite security, despite budgetary concerns during a period when the coronavirus pandemic has decimated revenues and limited programming.

These and other plantation sites are under scrutiny by critics demanding accountability and a better approach to interpreting history, one that eschews the Romanticism of the past in favor of a harsh reckoning long overdue. Managers at these historic sites say they are ready for the challenge.

Positive change

Many historic antebellum sites, damaged during the Civil War, were brought back to life in the first part of the 1900s as private hunting grounds or retreats used by family descendants or new owners investing in property down South. In time, some of these sites became public spaces, sharing their gardens, majestic live oaks, river views and old houses with paying customers. A combination of park and museum, they tended to emphasize the aesthetic beauty of the landscape over the yet-to-be-excavated history of slavery.

A few properties were developed into multiuse public spaces by private owners. Magnolia Plantation and Gardens, a sprawling site along the Ashley River, offers visitors opportunities to enjoy the grounds, learn about its history, or hold on-site events. Lowndes Grove on the Charleston peninsula is primarily an event venue operated by Patrick Properties. Boone Hall Plantation in Mount Pleasant offers history tours, hosts events and operates a working farm.

Other sites were transformed into nonprofit organizations or foundations increasingly dedicated to sharing their histories. By the 1970s, Middleton Place and Drayton Hall were nonprofits committed to historic preservation and interpretation. Patrons could admire the collection of objects in the house, stroll through a manicured landscape, interact with farm animals, watch demonstrations on blacksmithing, or learn about rice cultivation, the agricultural expertise of enslaved West Africans, and the brutality of bondage.

In recent decades, more and more has been presented at these sites to pay tribute to those whose forced labor enabled white planters to accumulate enormous wealth. Some white visitors reluctant to confront the realities of slavery pushed back. But now, as the country grapples with persistent police violence and entrenched discrimination against African Americans, many wonder whether historic plantation sites are doing enough, or whether they continue to hold tightly to old thinking and old practices that prioritize tourism income over a long-overdue national reckoning.

Administrators at local nonprofit sites say they welcome the reckoning as well as opportunities to be part of the solution.

"Middleton Place Foundation connects people to the past, inspiring a deeper understanding of ourselves and American history," President and CEO Tracey Todd said of the mission. "That's positive change if that could happen."

Carter Hudgins, president and CEO of Drayton Hall, said the key word is "reverence."

"How do we establish appropriate reverence for the history of a given site?" he asked. "We take much more of an archaeological approach ... in the sense that we are studying and interpreting the remains of past human activity. So the house can be looked at as an archaeological artifact. We want to know how things were made, how they were used, who made them."

It's about acknowledging the total history of the site, not giving preference to one group over others, he said.

Both leaders added that, to properly appreciate the institution of slavery, one must develop an understanding of the slavers and the way they lived, and vice versa. The lives of white planters and the lives of those they enslaved are inextricably intertwined.

McLeod Plantation, a relatively modest property that's part of the Charleston County Park and Recreation Commission, takes a different approach. Located in a densely populated suburban environment, the former Sea Island cotton plantation has little but a row of preserved slave cabins, an avenue of oaks and a small exhibit in the old plantation house. Recently, it became a member of the International Coalition of Sites of Conscience.

As a county park site, it receives about half of its annual budgeted income from government sources, and it caters to locals, according to Shawn Halifax, cultural history interpretation coordinator for the park commission.

"The theme is focused on how enslaved people and their descendants experienced the transition to freedom," Halifax said. "(We are) trying to make (an) effort to collaborate with descendant communities to work with them to program the site."

The historical emphasis, in other words, is entirely on the African and African American experience.

Wanting the truth

McLeod was operated by middle-class white farmers. Drayton Hall and Middleton Place, instead, were seats of power for influential families that included political leaders, prominent religious figures, a signer of the Declaration of Independence and others with proven historical bona fides.

Todd said much work has been done at Middleton Place over the years to uncover and record aspects of the Black experience at the main plantation and several others owned by the Middleton family. That work is perhaps underappreciated by critics focused only on slavery and its horrors.

"Part of that might be our own fault," Todd mused. "Is there an appetite to listen? A lot of people are looking for villains these days."

But the ancient magnolia tree, nurtured by generations of enslaved people, also is part of the history of this place, he noted.

"We've got to keep doing what we do, but better and more thoughtfully," Todd said.

That could mean more family reunions that include African Americans descendants of enslaved laborers at Middleton Place, more exhibits, new video testimonies, artistic interpretations of slavery, more research, more articles and documentaries or more public outreach and engagement.

"Middleton Place is, if you think about it, a monument to West African people," Todd said, for it was Africans who created it. "It's probably the most enduring monument to West African people that exists in this country."

Colin Quashie, an African American artist based in Charleston whose work often examines entrenched racism, said displaying the opulence enjoyed by white people in the antebellum period does not bother him, but such splendor must be put into context.

"The biggest issue I have with (plantations) is the focus," Quashie said. "It should be a much more sobering response, instead of this celebratory response."

It's wrong to emphasize the majesty of the big house and the beauty of the gardens over the *source* of all that wealth.

"I just don't understand the difficulty in telling the truth and putting things in perspective," he said. "I don't understand why it's such a moral dilemma to say the horrors on the outside paid for the opulence on the inside. Make the contrast clearer."

And, yeah, do away with the weddings.

"Would Germans allow people to have a wedding at Auschwitz?"

Quashie said he appreciates that these sites require money to operate and interpret history, but surely there are other sources of income besides weddings and parties. For example, the community might support a new tourism tax, or a new real estate impact fee earmarked for a cultural preservation fund.

"See how swiftly they moved to take Calhoun down?" Quashie said, referring to the removal of the John C. Calhoun monument in Marion Square on June 24. Plantation sites should move just as fast, and set the standard for other institutions to follow, he said. "There is a groundswell of people wanting the truth."

Hudgins said Drayton Hall, which is owned by the National Trust for Historic Preservation and operated by the Drayton Hall Preservation Trust, hasn't hosted a wedding for almost 10 years. The topic of on-site weddings came up last year, and the staff considered the need for new revenues, but decided against reintroducing such events. They were accustomed to the absence of wedding revenue, and chose to emphasize "authentic interpretation and stewardship" instead.

"As stewards of these sites, we need to do a better job at acknowledging the contributions of enslaved African Americans," he said. "That's why the archaeology is so important, because you can grasp the tangible and intangible stories of everybody who worked at Drayton Hall. … What's so important to understand is the work we're doing is not preserving white supremacy; we're preserving the collective history of the Lowcountry to better understand ourselves."

More of the story

Some who are engaged in the debate about the value and purpose of historic plantations have cited the example of the Whitney Plantation in Louisiana, which opened in late 2014.

"Whitney Plantation Museum is the only museum in Louisiana with an exclusive focus on the lives of enslaved people," its website states. "During your visit, you will learn about the history of slavery on a southern Louisiana sugarcane plantation by visiting memorials built to honor enslaved people; as well as original slave cabins, a freedmen's church, detached kitchen, and a 1790 owner's house."

"The Whitney is a large exhibit," noted Todd. An old plantation was transformed into a big memorial. "Middleton Place is a real 18th-century landscape created by African Americans. It's different. … Middleton Place is trying to tell more of the story."

Lester said he appreciates the effort.

"Could they do more? Probably. But are they sweeping that under the rug? By no means, and I saw that," he said.

The docents and interpreters didn't avoid the subject of slavery; they explained freely what life was like for Black people at Middleton Place, according to Lester.

"I wasn't getting a skewed version," he said.

A decade ago, during a visit to the site, Lester and his family were the only African Americans on the slavery tour during which the guide spoke about how, during Gen. William Tecumseh Sherman's advance, Union troops burned the main house and north flanker.

"Someone in the group said that was so tragic," Lester recalled. "The docent winked at my wife and I and said there were other tragic things that happened here. I have to tip my hat to that."

Preserving history

About a year ago, Lester was at Drayton Hall for a tour when the guide talked about how slaves have existed for thousands of years, seeming to belittle the "peculiar institution" of American slavery. He spoke up, asking that from now on the guide be certain to distinguish between ancient servitude, which often was part of a class system, and the transatlantic slave trade, a uniquely cruel episode in history that purposefully transformed Black people into property and excluded them from participating in social and economic systems.

"I have two daughters," he said. "I just wanted them to know their history. When I think of people who are my heroes, it's slaves, people who survived."

Though much progress has been made improving the presentation of history at former plantation sites, there's still a little "Gone with the Wind" nostalgia that permeates these places, Lester added. It's past time to extinguish the nostalgia.

"Tell a more transparent story," he reiterated. "That, I'd say, is the ask."

To do so, it would help to have more African Americans on staff, doing the research and sharing history with the public, he said.

"Why can't African Americans give tours? Are you going to HBCUs? There are people you can groom," he said.

Another improvement would entail making bifurcated tours obsolete. Visitors should not be able to choose between, say, the House Tour and the Slavery Tour, Lester said. Every tour should include a full discussion of slavery.

Generally, though, these sites are striving to do better. Their importance is unquestionable, Lester said.

"There is, I think, a place for them," Lester said. "If for some reason they didn't exist, there's a lot of history that African Americans want to know that would disappear."

October 17, 2020

Why Highways Were Designed to Run through Black Communities

In 1965, the house at 270 Ashley Ave. was bulldozed.

This was no ordinary Charleston house. This was the home of J. Arthur Brown, president of the South Carolina NAACP. This was where NAACP attorneys Thurgood Marshall and Matthew Perry stayed when they were in town, and where civil rights and political leaders such as Herbert Fielding, Roy Wilkins and Harry Belafonte's first wife, Marguerite Belafonte, found sanctuary.

This was the place where plans were laid — to integrate the Charleston County public schools, to join the Kress sit-ins — where the civil rights movement pulsated strongly in Charleston. This was a house in the heart of a mostly Black, mostly self-sufficient community during the period of legalized segregation.

"We literally were a prime example of the strength that communities bring forth, because it wasn't about closing off and fencing off," said Brown's daughter Millicent Brown. "There was this cross-fertilization that comes because you have people of different backgrounds, income and education levels, but intermingling."

Then came the surveyors, the heavy equipment, the cement.

Then Brown's neighborhood was split in two.

At least 150 homes disappeared to make way for "The Crosstown," a six-lane highway connecting Interstate 26 with the Ashley River Bridge.

Flash-forward to 2020. The Phillips community, a settlement of African Americans who can trace their lineage to slavery times, faces the prospect of a road-widening project that is certain to weaken an already tenuous hold on their inherited land. The Phillips community, divided by S.C. Highway 41, now is the focus of an intensifying debate about the impacts of residential and economic growth, and an imbalance of political power that favors wealthy, mostly White homeowners over their Black neighbors.

In the Charleston region, several road projects have impacted Black neighborhoods. Highway projects such as the construction of I-26 into the Charleston peninsula, and the adjoining Crosstown, were part of an effort that compromised African American communities, according to residents and scholars.

Numerous road projects were undertaken nationwide in the 1950s and 1960s as part of the federal interstate highway program. Project managers knew their roads would damage and divide Black communities, pursuing them in the name of "slum clearance" or "urban renewal," according to Richard Rothstein, author of "The Color of Law." Constructing highways became an excuse for the large-scale transfer of Black populations.

Slum clearance reinforced segregation and impoverishment, making it ever more difficult for Black families to find their way to the middle class, Rothstein wrote.

Other projects changed Black neighborhoods incrementally and indirectly, not because their architects wanted to inflict harm, but because these areas provided the path of least resistance.

Policymakers must weigh and balance competing priorities, said Maren Trochmann, professor of political science and public administration at the College of Charleston, who spent years working for the federal Housing and Urban Development agency. "In the Lowcountry, this is complicated by ... the history of land loss among African Americans," she said.

Decisions often are made in good faith, but our socioeconomic system favors the privileged and powerful over the disenfranchised, Trochmann said.

"Policymakers now should be aware of this history, but then determining how you make right decades of racist housing policy, redlining, and interstate highway construction that destroyed that ability of Black people to accrue wealth — that's another problem," Trochmann said.

Folly Road and 41

Sixty years ago, the city of Charleston was contained to the peninsula. Highways tended to have two lanes. Cross the Ashley River and you were soon in the country. Cross the Cooper River and you found the small town of Mount Pleasant, beyond which were African American residential enclaves and mom-and-pop shops along U.S. Highway 17.

Daniel Island? Undeveloped. James Island? A stretch of land that was half-suburban, half rural.

Bill "Cubby" Wilder, 75, drove a bus along Folly Road when it was two dusty lanes. In the late-1800s, Wilder's great-grandfather bought land on the Sol Legare Island, nestled in the marsh that separates the mainland from Folly Beach. It was a farming and fishing community then.

Wilder said he grew up in a segregated bubble — until the nearby beach, which featured a famous pier and pavilion that was open only to White people, began to draw visitors, along with African Americans who found low-wage jobs in the emerging tourist economy. In the summer of 1920, a private toll road and causeway made of sand, clay and gravel opened to automobiles. It cut across Wilder's island, separating most of the residents from the Stem Point Memorial Cemetery where their dead were buried.

Residents living near the new roadway complained about the dust churned up by the passing cars. So, in 1926, Charleston County applied a thin layer of asphalt, then thickened it little by little in subsequent years, Charleston County Public Library historian Nic Butler said. In 1955, work began to widen the road to four lanes. In 1971, County Council and the state's Department of Transportation approved adding a fifth lane.

In the 1960s, Ocean Plaza opened, with its arcade games, Ferris Wheel and other rides, eateries and shops. Wilder's mother found domestic work there. His father, a fisherman, sold shrimp to the stores.

As Folly Road widened, development ramped up and traffic increased, putting pressure on the Sol Legare community, he said. Under the leadership of Mayor Joe Riley, the city began to annex much of James Island, growing its tax base. As more subdivisions were built, property values increased.

"More and more people were moving to the area, so the old way of life faded," Wilder said.

In 1989, Hurricane Hugo inflicted terrible damage along the Low-country coast. Many Black families could not afford to rebuild and meet new elevation requirements. They didn't have home insurance, and the Federal Emergency Management Agency wasn't much help, Wilder said.

"All these Black communities are being affected by overdevelopment and ... (too much) growth, because they didn't provide the infrastructure — our government didn't do that," he said.

East of the Cooper River, a dirt road once wended its way around the Phillips community, providing access to several old plantations.

"The road circled around so everyone could get in and out," said community leader Richard Habersham.

In the 1940s, state workers rerouted it straight through the Phillips community and paved the arrow-straight two-lane street we see today. That did damage enough, but traffic in the evening was light.

"At night, we would sit on the road," Habersham said. "It was something we couldn't change, but we dealt with it."

As the economy heated up, largely thanks to the old Naval Shipyard, traffic became a serious issue by the 1960s, he said. Drivers sped along Highway 41 at 65 mph. It became perilous to cross the road.

When the Amoco plant was built along the Wando River, just to the north, traffic got worse. It included more trucks, more noise, more pollution, Habersham said. In the late-1980s, the massive Dunes West project got under way, with its golf course, tennis courts, swimming pool and big houses, followed in the 1990s by the Rivertowne on the Wando development on the other side of the highway. The people of the Phillips community, squeezed between these sprawling new residential developments, knew they would never again enjoy the peace and quiet of the old days.

The current plan for Highway 41 would widen the road to five lanes and, if "Alternative 1" is adopted, eminent domain would be used to appropriate private property and secure the right of way. Phillips residents would receive just compensation for their lost property, though many of the people living in the community, founded in 1875, are beneficiaries of what's called heirs property, owned outright and handed down through generations. These homes often have no clear deeds or named individual owners, which means securing government compensation could require legal interventions residents cannot afford and that might not succeed, Habersham said.

In any case, the money probably would not be enough to enable residents, who don't have mortgages and don't pay rent, to relocate nearby, Habersham said.

The widening project is controversial for other reasons. Engineers have noted that traffic at certain intersections likely will worsen, not improve, and the new roadway could further erode community cohesion.

What's more, studies show that wider roadways generally do not reduce traffic, they merely accommodate more vehicles. And adding new roads simply increases the amount of miles people travel in their cars. Every road has a natural congestion level that might be alleviated temporarily by widening projects, but always will return to its previous level, according to a 2011 report issued by the American Economic Association.

It's possible that officials will decide to route the roadway around the Phillips community, running it along the edge of Laurel Hill County Park to Dunes West Boulevard. This option, called "Alternative 7A," would be more expensive and could include sound barriers to protect Dunes West residents. A Highway 41 presentation to Charleston County Council was postponed until some time in November.

Policy and the law

After World War II, a concerted effort was made to develop the suburbs, and to build the infrastructure needed to sustain them. The low-density residential areas were meant for White homeowners only. Neighborhood associations, with the government's blessing, inserted segregationist clauses into their by-laws, and the Federal Housing Authority also imposed racial restrictions, Rothstein wrote.

The Federal Housing Acts of 1949 and 1954 and the Federal Highway Act of 1956 provided money and other incentives to cities for the purpose of demolishing blighted neighborhoods.

The practice of redlining designated certain predominantly Black neighborhoods ineligible for home loans, which degraded them economically and helped turn them into the "slums" that federal authorities chose to "clear," often in order to build highways.

It happened in most major U.S. cities — New Orleans, Houston, Detroit, New York City, Boston and San Francisco — and in smaller cities, too, such as Spartanburg and Columbia. These laws and practices have since been deemed unjust and are no longer in use, but the impacts of decades of road building and redlining still can be felt today.

Jeff Tibbals, a Mount Pleasant-based eminent domain and property rights attorney, said the law is not very good at addressing the concerns of individual communities.

In the early days of highway construction, budgetary pressures propelled engineers and contractors to work quickly, without much regard for environmental concerns, Tibbals said.

"Oftentimes, Black communities were in the path of least resistance. That's not to say there weren't good reasons to place these roads there. But the design was based on the individual rights of landowners, and not communities."

It took new legislation, such as the 1970 National Environmental Policy Act, to require road builders to examine social and environmental impacts, he said.

Real estate development generates commercial activity. Homeowners want easy access to dry cleaners, convenience stores, clothing outlets and restaurants. This increases the tax base, which incentivizes public officials to pursue growth as an economic strategy, and laying a road through a poor, semi-rural area is far cheaper than building it through a densely populated one, Tibbals said.

"Money talks, and sometimes poor communities with less don't have a voice," he said.

But community engagement can be tricky, Trochmann noted. Too often, for the bureaucrats, it's just a box to check, she said. And mobilizing communities to participate in public meetings can require more than an invitation. Will child care be provided? Translators? Transportation?

Strategic planning

Chad Long, director of environmental services at the S.C. Department of Transportation, said road projects differ depending on which agency is in charge and what impacts are predicted. The old practice of slum clearance effectively ceased, at least as official policy, in the 1970s, when NEPA was introduced, he said. And the 1966 National Historic Preservation Act protects certain areas, such as the Phillips community, that have received historical designation.

Today, agencies follow a defined review process, adhere to current regulations and seek to inform and engage local residents, often with multiple public meetings and community outreach, Long said.

Omar Muhammad, executive director of the Lowcountry Alliance for Model Communities, said the residents of low-income African American neighborhoods already are isolated socially and economically, in large measure because of decades of government infrastructure projects. The social fabric has weakened, making them less able to defend themselves.

Muhammad, who is focused on the concerns of the mostly Black neighborhoods that comprise the southern part of North Charleston, is a strong advocate for a sustainable regional growth plan that improves public transportation and reduces traffic, encourages economic activity, and adds greenways for biking and walking — all while making social equity a priority.

"As a region, we need to start thinking about growth beyond any single community," he said.

Today, Millicent Brown's childhood stomping grounds are changing again. The neighborhood divided by the Crosstown, officially renamed the Septima P. Clark Parkway in 2010 to pay tribute to the indomitable civil rights leader, is becoming more diverse. It's buzzing with commerce.

As always, the economic forces at play solve old problems and create new ones. Overt racism is uncommon now. But the racial implications of gentrification cause some civic leaders and residents to shiver with a sense of déjà vu.

For Brown, the old neighborhood was a model community, imperfect to be sure, but enriched by its economic diversity and the devotion neighbors showed one another.

Late one night in 1960, the Ku Klux Klan threw a burning cross into Brown's yard and set the house's front awning on fire. People nearby quickly extinguished the flames. The family received bomb threats and harassing telephone calls.

"We were an identified place," Brown said. This was a house with symbolism. It represented the aspirations of the entire community.

Then the highway came through. Residents abandoned their homes, and those with some means — the doctors and dentists, shop owners and schoolteachers — relocated.

J. Arthur Brown, a pragmatic businessman and civil rights leader, had developed a stiff upper jaw. He was not easily shaken, even by threats of violence against him and his family. But this was something different, a seismic force that could not be easily controlled.

"One of the only times I saw my father cry was when we knew we would lose the house, and learned how much we'd get for it," Millicent Brown recalled.

This was the house her grandfather built in 1920. This was where social justice activists gathered, where members of the community turned when they needed advice.

The Brown family received $25,000. They were among the more fortunate. They could relocate to family-owned property on James Island.

Their old neighborhood, once a safe haven for Black people in Charleston, became a shadow of itself.

"That is how you create a ghetto," Brown said.

The economic pendulum is swinging, though. Property values are way up, home renovations and new construction are common, families are moving in. And a new greenway project, the Lowcountry Lowline, promises to stitch back together the area divided by Interstate 26, providing a pedestrian and bike path, amenities and perhaps opportunities for neighborhood entrepreneurs.

Local government officials, and even some developers, have become more attuned to smart urban growth, pushing for more density, mixed-use communities, diversity and a focus on people's needs.

And residents throughout the Lowcountry have awakened to long-simmering racial tensions, joining national calls for social justice and adding to a chorus of defenders of the Phillips community.

In Martin Luther King Jr.'s vision of the Beloved Community, where solidarity trumps bigotry and discrimination, all people, no matter their station, have access to the wealth of the world.

To get there, though, we'll need good roads.

The Extraordinary Achievement of South Carolina's Holocaust Survivors

A generation of survivors mostly has vanished. Few are left to tell their stories.

No longer can they remind us about what happened in the camps and ghettos, on the transports and death marches. We cannot listen to their accounts of family trauma, firing squads, frozen flesh, resistance.

Many of Charleston's Holocaust survivors are gone. Pincus and Renee Kolender are gone. Charles Markowitz is gone. Margot Freudenberg is gone. Leon and Guta Blass Weintraub are gone. Rose Goldberg is gone. Others, too.

But their children and grandchildren are with us, and this simple fact reveals something important about the legacy of so many Holocaust survivors. The beginning of their lives was defined by suffering and loss. After the war, they sought normalcy — and, for the most part, achieved it.

They established themselves in a new place, learned a new language, joined a community, started careers, raised children, became grandparents. They created opportunity for themselves and generations to come.

"The survivors were reluctant heroes," said Martin Perlmutter, retired director of the Jewish Studies Program at the College of Charleston. "Their charge was to succeed in family life, in business and in community life. Their mantras of 'Never Again' and 'Tikkun Olam' (repair the world) were an affirmation of the importance of that normalcy. And their incredible success against overwhelming odds is their enduring legacy."

Luck of the draw

Larry Freudenberg's father, Henry, was 10 years old when, on the night of Nov. 9, 1938, German paramilitary forces, joined by many civilians, destroyed synagogues and Jewish businesses throughout the country and arrested 30,000 men.

The Freudenberg family had been hit hard — first by the economic depression, which destroyed H&L Freudenberg Department Store in the city of Essen, and then by the war. Even before Kristallnacht, Jewish schools were closed and the imperiled lives of Germany's Jewish residents were circumscribed.

Henry and his parents Margot and Walter already were in hiding and would remain out of sight for several more months. Then, in May 1939, before the German invasion of Poland that fall, the family managed to escape to London, where Margot had family.

But London was not safe, so the children in the city were sent to the countryside, including Henry.

Then, a stroke of luck. The U.S. was limiting the number of Jewish war refugees who could enter the country, requiring domestic sponsorship and administering a lottery system. The Freudenbergs were called. And a man in New York City who once worked for the family in Essen agreed to sponsor them.

Margot had a sister who, many years earlier, had moved to Greenville. A Jewish organization placing survivors and refugees sent the family to Charleston and found them an apartment on King Street. It was 1940. Soon, the Triest family, active at Kahol Kadosh Beth Elohim synagogue, would invite the Freudenberg's over for dinner. Henry, now 11, met Maxine, 10, for the first time.

Walter ran a shop on King Street but died from diabetes in 1952. Margot became a prominent physical therapist in Charleston and, in 1970, founded the Hope Lodge, a temporary residence for cancer patients.

Henry and Maxine started dating in high school and eventually married. Henry attended The Citadel, entered the Army and years later retired, full of pride, a full colonel. In 1953, he went to work for his in-laws, who operated an insurance agency.

They had three children, including Larry, who is now 61 and the owner of the Triest Agency.

"I grew up as an American kid," he said.

His father had divorced himself from anything German and refused to consider himself a "Holocaust survivor." That term was reserved for those who had been deported to labor and death camps, he had insisted.

Grandma's house

Lilly Filler's Polish parents, Jadzia Sklarz and Ben Stern, both survived several concentration camps. Ben lasted about eight months, shuttling between six locations, before he was liberated in April 1945. Jadzia lasted 21 months, and was liberated in May 1945.

Of Ben's family of six, only he and an older sister survived. Of Jadzia's family of 10, only she and two older siblings survived.

Ben and Jadzia met in Munich after the war. They married in June 1946. Lilly was born in December 1947. They wanted to leave Europe badly. Ben remembered uncle Gabe who had emigrated to Lexington, S.C., in 1918. He reached out. Upon arrival in Lexington, Gabe Stern put Ben to work in his retail shop.

"This was not his cup of tea," Filler said. Ben's English was limited, along with his familiarity with American culture. But his work ethic was strong. In the camps, Ben had been a carpenter and that experience soon would come in handy.

Thanks to the generosity of a local man, Ben found a job at a lumber supply company. He quickly learned the language and customs of his new home. After five years, he opened his own construction company, which specialized at first in homebuilding, then got a commercial contract to build 7-Eleven stores. The business transformed into a commercial real estate enterprise and then a development company.

Filler said her mother Jadzia never lost her "strong" accent and never fully assimilated into American culture. But she was just as determined to succeed as her husband. She enrolled in college courses and mastered domestic skills.

"My parents were very loving," Filler said. "They did not speak of the horrors, did not have hate in their heart."

To Filler, the family seemed normal enough.

"What I began to understand as I turned a little bit older was that we didn't have an extended family — no grandparents, aunts or uncles, cousins," she said.

At elementary school, her teacher would ask the students about their weekends and invariably some would mention visits to their grandparent's house.

"I came home and asked my mom, 'Can we go to grandma's house for dinner?'"

Filler had no concept of what "grandma" meant. Was it a place, a restaurant perhaps?

"A grandma is a family member, and you don't have one," her mother explained.

Filler recalled how her mother, tormented by nightmares, would scream in the dark. Every night. Her terrors would awaken the household and cause her younger children to cry in distress.

"When I met my dad in the hallway, he would say, 'You go take care of your brothers, and I'll go take care of your mother.' I didn't know until college that that was not normal. It was the only residual that I saw, other than the tattoos."

As the oldest child, Filler was protective of her parents, and an overachiever, she said. She would go on to become a doctor of obstetrics and gynecology.

Ben and Jadzia, resilient and possessing a strong faith and commitment to the community, ultimately would be blessed with 11 grandchildren.

Keeping up the fight

Fred Volkman's mother, Susan, watched as her family was taken to the camps. She and an uncle managed to find their way to a small Polish ghetto, but ran into trouble and went into hiding for years.

Volkman's father, Michael, and his family were arrested and all but Michael and his brother Larry were transported to the death camps. The two young men instead ended up in a labor camp. The German authorities suspected Michael of collaborating with the Polish underground, detained and tortured him for three days. But Michael said nothing and went back to work.

That winter, the brothers were shipped by rail on crowded cattle cars to a concentration camp, stripped naked in the freezing cold and told to prepare for a shower. They had heard the rumors. Would they be pushed into a gas chamber?

No, it was a routine delousing treatment. They would live another day.

Some detainees plotted an escape, which embarrassed the German camp commander. In retaliation, he lined up all the prisoners and shot every tenth one.

The brothers were transferred to the Flossenburg camp in Bavaria, where workers were building fighter planes. Larry contracted typhus and died.

When, in 1945, the Allies approached the camp, the Germans loaded their prisoners into cattle cars, climbed atop the train, and rolled away. An American Army unit noticed the fleeing Germans perched on the roof of the train cars and opened fire, killing many, including some inside, Volkman recounted. Soon, the Americans blew up the tracks, stranding the train. Armed German soldiers forced their prisoners to embark on a death march; anyone who collapsed or attempted to flee would be shot.

"Dad decided he would either die in the march, or die trying to escape," Volkman said. He ran and was hit twice in the neck. Michael woke up in a Red Cross barracks where a Jewish-American corporal enlisted his services.

First, dressed as a German POW, he would join the other POWs and listen to their conversations, hoping to glean information about where members of the Nazi leadership were located. He delivered aid to displaced-persons camps and even joined a theater troupe, his son said.

At one of the camps, he recognized someone he knew: Susan's uncle. And then Susan appeared. It was love at first sight. Michael found various excuses to return to the camp.

Then, Susan and her uncle left for Chicago. Michael remained in Germany, helping Jews find safe passage to Palestine and to England. He wanted to join the fight for Israeli independence, but Susan dissuaded him. He had seen enough war.

On the West Side of Chicago, he sold wares from a cart, eventually saving up enough money to open a small shop, but the business didn't thrive. Michael and Susan moved to the North Side, where many Holocaust survivors settled. They lived in a small, one-bedroom, walk-up apartment.

Fred Volkman, who came of age in the 1960s and embraced hippie culture, would take long walks with his father and talk about nearly everything, especially progressive politics. But the Holocaust rarely came up. It was many years later that Fred understood what those two marks on his father's neck were about.

Fred went on to medical school and became a pediatrician. His brother, a student of political science and business administration, went to work for state government. Larry died of cancer at age 29, a loss from which Susan would never recover.

Fred advanced in his career, became interested in population health and migrated to the business side of medicine, moving first to Georgia, then Texas. In 2007, after the three kids were grown, he and his wife Judy moved to Charleston.

The survivor's burden

Perlmutter said it was astounding that these survivors managed to recover a degree of normalcy in their lives. But most felt the weight of obligation upon their shoulders. Life could not be frittered away; one had to be productive, to give something back.

"Their burden was to make the world into a better place," Perlmutter said.

October 29, 2020

John Stroman, student leader of 1968 protests in Orangeburg, revisits All-Star Bowling Lanes

ORANGEBURG — Lane 1 always gave him problems. The wall to his left prevented him from finding just the right position to ensure the counterclockwise spin he put on the ball would propel it toward the pins with the finesse needed for a strike.

A well-aimed hook was easier to accomplish a lane or two to the right, and that's where John Stroman liked to be for his league nights — near the concessions, near the front door of All-Star Bowling Lanes.

The last time he bowled here was about 20 years ago. His black 16-pound ball, with his initials J.W.S. etched above the finger holes, sat on the rack when not in use. He'd left it there, even after he stopped going to the venue, even after it closed for good in 2007.

The ball collected dust.

But Stroman's memories of the bowling alley always have remained stark and immediate. For this was the place where he once led volatile student protests. Here was the place where police landed their batons on his head.

This was the scene in February 1968 when Black students from S.C. State College and Claflin University gathered to vent their frustration over segregation in Orangeburg, where they were met with violence and fear, where they ran the gauntlet.

Here, at the All-Star Bowling Lanes, was where the first events occurred in a confrontation that would culminate two days later in a burst of violence on campus.

Stroman was the student who started it all, and he has no reason to regret what he did.

Abandoned and languishing for 13 years now, the downtown bowling alley on Russell Street is being reclaimed thanks to an anonymous donor's gift. The donor purchased the property for $145,000 and transferred the deed to the Center for Creative Partnerships, which seeks to apply the arts and humanities to the fight for social justice and civil rights.

The center was started by Ellen Zisholtz in the 1990s. In January of this year she transformed it into a nonprofit, and soon assembled a board of directors, and then a project advisory board. Now it must raise the money for the renovation work.

The goal is to restore the bowling lanes and to create a museum and learning center devoted to the Orangeburg Massacre and the events leading up to that first-ever campus shooting in the U.S. involving law enforcement.

If all goes as planned, the Orangeburg All-Star Justice Center will include several operational bowling lanes, an exhibition space, a venue for public gatherings and discussion, informational displays, interactive features and possibly an outdoor movie screen where documentaries and relevant feature films can be shown, Zisholtz said.

Joining 'The Cause'

Stroman, tall, lean and unsteady on his feet at 77 years old, is back inside the bowling alley, listening, remembering. The ball-carrying equipment is in pieces. Old advertisements are mounted above each lane. The carpet is damp and smells of mold.

The ghosts of the segregated past still hover in the air. All the bustle and change since 1968 — the dropped pins, the noise and camaraderie of league nights — can't quite drown out the sounds of police sirens and cries of pain.

When he was 15, growing up in Savannah, he worked as a pin boy at a local bowling alley. After his shift in the evenings, he and his friends would hop on their bikes to ride home. Sometimes White teenagers in their cars would follow them, rolling down their windows to shout epithets and taunts, or to toss something at the Black boys pedaling furiously to escape their abusers.

On one occasion, one of the White boys, wielding a belt, leaned too far out the window and fell from the car. Stroman and his friends hardly looked back; they knew they would be blamed for the injuries the White teen sustained. So Stroman quit his job at the bowling alley.

In March 1960, when he was 17, he witnessed the start of what would become a 19-month boycott of White-owned businesses downtown. The city's Black residents, led by the NAACP, challenged segregation first at the retail lunch counters, then throughout Savannah, until, in October 1961, city officials opened the parks, pools, restaurants, retail shops and buses to all.

In 1963, during his first year in Orangeburg, where he had joined one of his brothers and enrolled at S.C. State College, Stroman was among hundreds of students who sought to join a protest march through the downtown commercial district, but police were there to greet them. Several protesters were beaten and around 400 arrested. Stroman and many others spent two weeks in jail.

By the middle of his sophomore year, his grades were suffering. It didn't help that Stroman was quick to reject school rules he considered unfair. He was gaining a reputation as a troublemaker. He took time off from school and moved to New York City, staying with a brother and converting to Islam, giving up cigarettes, pork and alcohol for the rest of his life.

But he wasn't one to quit hardship, so he returned to Orangeburg — to his school work, his friends and his protests.

In February 1967, he was one of three students who demonstrated in front of college President Benner C. Turner's home on campus. The students objected to the dismissal of three capable White professors, to the structure and discipline imposed on the school's young people, to the dress code and compulsory chapel attendance, and to what was called the Berlin Wall — a tall barbed-wire fence separating Claflin and S.C. State, which had been constructed after the protests of the early '60s.

The unrest soon expanded across the campus and became known as "The Cause." A young organizer with the Student Nonviolent Coordinating Committee, Cleveland Sellers, traveled to Orangeburg to advise students, advocate for fair policies and more Black studies programming. He also promoted the formation of the Black Awareness Coordinating Committee, which Stroman promptly joined.

For his activism, Stroman was expelled from school. But the die had been cast. Gov. Robert McNair negotiated an effective settlement, and pressure was placed on Turner to step down. By the fall of 1967, many of the students' demands were met, Turner was replaced by a far more sympathetic M. Maceo Nance, and students ejected from the school were re-admitted.

Sellers, by then a Black Power proponent closely associated with the firebrand orator and SNCC chairman Stokely Carmichael, was perceived by the conservative White establishment of Orangeburg as a threat — though his focus was cultural and educational. He wanted young Black people to push for change by unshackling their minds, embracing their history and awakening to the interconnectedness of oppressive regimes around the world. His agenda was that of self-determination and self-empowerment.

Stroman, instead, wanted to bowl.

Initial challenge

For years, Black people in Orangeburg sought access to All-Star Bowling Lanes, but its management kept the venue segregated. Black bowlers were forced to drive nearly an hour to Columbia.

In October 1967, Stroman was singularly obsessed with ending segregation at the local bowling alley. Sellers, quickly labeled the "outside agitator" by authorities though he hailed from nearby Denmark and contemplated enrolling at S.C. State, returned to Orangeburg to continue his advocacy work on campus and rally support for BACC. The two men generally did not see eye to eye.

Stroman soon found an opportunity to challenge the new owner of All-Star Bowling Lanes, Harry Floyd. The lanky activist was approached by fellow student James Davis, who had returned from six years in the Air Force only to discover he was still prohibited from patronizing the nearby bowling lanes. Davis wanted to take action.

Stroman, back in Savannah for the holidays, could not get the idea out of his head.

"All I could hear was 'bowling alley, bowling alley, bowling alley,'" he said.

He visited a venue in his hometown and explained the problem to the White owner.

"Do they have a lunch counter?" the owner asked. If so, even a private business could be subject to the interstate commerce clause of the U.S. Constitution, making it illegal for them to segregate by race.

Stroman and Davis devised a scheme, recounted in the book "The Orangeburg Massacre" by Jack Bass and Jack Nelson. They would ask S.C. State's only White student to be a foil. He would go to the bowling alley on Monday, Jan. 29, followed by a small group of Black patrons who would then challenge the assertion that the venue was a "privately owned club." If an unknown White student who was not a club member could gain entry, why not the Black students?

Oscar Butler, dean of men at the college, learned of the effort and went to observe. About a dozen young people sat at the lunch counter and were ignored. When they asked for lanes, they were told the bowling alley was a private club. The students pointed to their White friend, who was immediately ordered to stop bowling. Floyd told the group to leave, but they resisted, hoping the owner would call the police. They played music on the jukebox and purchased soft drinks from a vending machine.

Then Floyd insisted that Butler escort the students out.

Stroman conveyed the incident to BACC, but the student group was concerned with other matters. He wrote a letter to the American Bowling Congress, reporting the discrimination and asking for intervention. The reply was disappointing. The organization would do nothing.

One week later, on Monday, Feb. 5, league night, about 15 young people showed up at All-Star Bowling Lanes.

"We came to bowl, man!" someone said as he entered the building.

"This is a private business!" came the reply.

"We're tired of 'private,' we're coming in!"

Every small item touched by an African American was tossed in the garbage, Stroman said. A student wrapped his arms around the juke box. "Throw this away!" came the challenge.

That's when Floyd called the authorities.

Orangeburg Police Chief Roger Poston showed up and told Floyd he'd need to secure arrest warrants in order to take action. The city ordered the bowling alley closed for the night, and about a dozen protesters were forced to leave.

The confrontation was escalating, and on the next night it devolved into violence and bloodshed.

'A lot of hate'

The law was muddy. Was Floyd exempted from the requirements of the Civil Rights Act because of his business' private status, or did Black protesters have a right to patronize the venue? The city decided to side with Floyd.

When Stroman returned Tuesday evening with another group of students, they were met by around 20 police officers, including members of the state Highway Patrol deployed by Chief J.P. (Pete) Strom of the State Law Enforcement Division. Strom told the young student leader that trespassers would be arrested, but it would only take one or two arrests to trigger a court case that challenged Floyd's policy.

Word spread to keep cool and disperse, especially after about 15 students were handcuffed.

That might have been the end of it, but someone rushed to campus and told students watching a movie about the arrests at the bowling alley. Enraged, hundreds made their way to the venue, where the situation soon spiraled out of control.

A small group burst into the venue but were forced out after about 25 minutes. A renewed effort to disperse the crowd in an orderly fashion nearly took hold, then fell apart when a firetruck pulled into the parking lot. Students were quickly reminded of a 1960 confrontation during which students were repelled with firehoses.

"Where's the fire?" they taunted, waving cigarette lighters.

Stroman stood atop a car and urged the students to leave. Another 50 officers arrived. First they moved near the firetruck to protect it as it pulled away, but students surged in the direction of the venue, so officers rushed after them. Windows shattered. A student was arrested. Another sprayed something caustic into the eyes of an officer. Pushing and shoving quickly led to the swinging of batons.

Students, many of them young women, were injured. Stroman was struck on the head. On their way back to campus, some shattered shop windows with bricks.

"That's what galvanized the student body," said Bill Hine, a retired history professor who taught at S.C. State. "If things had dissipated that night, maybe nothing much would have happened."

The next day was tense. McNair called in the National Guard. FBI agents maneuvered quietly through the city, keeping an eye on Sellers. State troopers established a center of operations just outside the main entrance of S.C. State College. The city was on lockdown, its White residents warned of impending riots.

Two young White men sped onto campus in their car, firing gunshots from the windows, then driving into a dead-end. They spun around and sped away. Two Black students felt the sting of birdshot as they took a common shortcut to campus through a private yard.

Negotiations in the city failed to diffuse the tension. Frustrated students were confined to campus.

Thursday night — Feb. 8, 1968 — a large group of unarmed students gathered on a bluff near the edge of the campus, lit a bonfire and confronted an army of local police, state troopers, National Guardsmen and military vehicles. Patrolmen under Strom's command lined up at the curb, guns loaded with buckshot aimed at the college students.

An officer's gun went off. A wooden bannister was thrown by a student, striking one of the officers in the face. And then, a little after 10:30 p.m., the buckshot hissed across the bluff and found the flesh of angry protestors. Many were struck in the back or the soles of their feet as they scrambled to escape the 8- to 10-second barrage.

Henry Smith was shot in the neck and shoulder. Delano Middleton was shot in the chest. Samuel Hammond was shot in the back. They died that night. At least 28 others were wounded.

Sellers had been struck near the armpit. At the hospital later, he was arrested on several charges, including inciting a riot. Stroman, though, was not there. He had gone to stay with his aunt on the west side of Orangeburg. He tried to get back onto the campus around 6 p.m. the day of the shooting, but was turned away.

He learned of the carnage at 7 the next morning, while listening to the radio.

"I wanted to kill everything in sight," he said. "I had a lot of hate in me."

'A big hole'

Stroman finished school, got certified in math, science and chemistry, married in 1970 and tried to find a job as a school teacher in Orangeburg. But no one would hire him, he said. Over the years, he would find work in Allendale, Denmark, Elloree and elsewhere.

Soon after the Orangeburg Massacre, Floyd opened his bowling alley to all, and Stroman was its first Black patron. He joined the league and appeared routinely, using his heavy engraved ball and avoiding Lane 1.

At the venue last week, he listened to Zisholtz describe the renovation plans. The dropped ceiling would go. The carpet would get ripped out. Big TV screens would be mounted over each working lane providing information about the civil rights movement. An interactive feature would display messages typed by visitors promising their commitment to social justice. A museum display would describe the historical significance of the bowling alley.

"It's really going to serve as an educational flagship," observed Anna Zacherl, who sits on the board of the Center for Creative Partnerships and who runs the Orangeburg County libraries.

Jermaine Middleton, an advisory board member and niece of Delano Middleton, one of the three students killed in 1968, said the project is a way to remember her uncle for generations.

"I don't know who my cousins would have been," she said, musing about the generational disruption the killing caused. "What was it like for my grandmother, who lost her youngest son? … I think about it a lot. … There's a big hole in our family."

Stroman is mostly silent, listening, thinking. He mentions he left his ball here two decades ago, just before the venue, which had been renamed All-Star Triangle Bowling, closed for good.

Zacherl turns on the flashlight of her mobile phone and examines the balls remaining on the racks. Suddenly, the initials J.W.S. are illuminated.

Stroman tests the finger holes to see if they fit.

And then he carries his ball away.

II.

RELIGION:
Confronting the Ways of Faith

Introduction

by the Rev. Bert Keller

"There is nothing more confusing or more complex than religion," says one of Adam's conversation partners in this eclectic, time-traveling collection of stories.

He is right, of course. Making a deep dive into the waters of religion brings to mind a line from an old Shaker hymn: *An ocean I see without bottom or shore.* Here's a subject matter without boundaries. You're plunging into fathomless depths of the human spirit, into astonishing leaps of human culture.

But that man's comment contains a subtle warning, too. The institutional embodiments of religion bristle with boundaries, "no trespassing" signs, emotional minefields that spell danger even for the careful diver. It is both aspects — the fascination and the risk-taking — that make a deep dive into the waters of religion such an exciting adventure.

These essays "report," but they go beyond reporting. They create, they interpret, they paint landscapes or mindscapes that take us there, to the heart of it. For example, "Magic... or Mystery?" lets conversation partners tell the story, but the author helps us make sense of the mind-challenging enigmas by giving a framework of research and comprehensive overview.

From the safe and shallow waters of American civil religion to the most exotic, eccentric beliefs held by our neighbors, here is a fresh take on them all. One with insight and with balance.

And with *respect*. I challenge the reader to find a judgmental slant in these essays. The author titles this section "confronting the ways of faith," but if confrontation implies denigration or argument, you won't find that here. What you *do* find: honest inquiry, turning issues over to examine them, genuine dialogue (subjectivity is never hidden from view, and it shouldn't be). In a word: Respect.

But what I like most, and I think you will too, is the sheer delight that animates every essay, every paragraph. Here's a writer loving what he's doing. Like a diver discovering a new coral reef teeming with incredible life, he can't conceal his pleasure in observing, questioning, interpreting. It is delight that animates these essays, the delight of the chase. And here at the outset I feel like saying: Can I come too?

The Rev. Bert Keller is former pastor of Circular Congregational Church.

December 10, 2006

Sold on a Saint

Oh Joe,
where do you go?
Down, down, down
in the cold, cold ground,

with your feet on top
and your head below.
As the porch light burns,
cars go to and fro.

And pushing time
is ol' St. Joe.

The prayer's been said,
the sellers wait.
An offer comes —
it's good, it's great!

A fast sale's made
as markets decline.

The sellers think
a force divine
p'raps intervened
to speed up time.

So to the site
of ol' St. Joe
with spade in hand
and happy glow.

For now it's time
to pull him out,
to turn him right,
to be devout.

For good ol' Joe,
saint of home and hearth
has shown his stuff,
has proved his worth.

You can order the kit online or buy the equipment *a la carte* at Pauline Books and Media on Charleston's lower King Street.

The testimonials are many. Homeowners and real estate agents are resorting to pleas for divine intervention in the effort to sell homes. The inspired instrument to be buried in the yard? St. Joseph. Hey, it can't hurt, they say.

And as residential real estate markets soften across the country, the little St. Joseph figurines, prepped for burial and packaged with ready-made prayers, are selling like hotcakes.

The practice

It is said that the practice of burying St. Joseph began centuries ago when an order of nuns in Spain wanted to secure land to build a convent. They buried a medallion of the saint, prayed and, sure enough, they got their land.

Eventually, the medallion was replaced with a statue whose purpose was to help sell, not claim, property.

Here's what you do: Procure a St. Joseph statuette. Wrap it in a protective covering. Bury it, upside down and facing the street, by your "For Sale" sign. Say a little prayer. And wait.

When your home sells a few days (weeks? months?) later, unearth your St. Joseph and put him in a place of honor in your new home.

It's in the saint's interest to expedite the sale. The sooner you close, the sooner St. Joseph sees the light.

Now, there are other ways to do it. Some people bury the figurine so it faces the house, not the street. Some bury it feet down. Some find a spot farther from the street. Owners of condos that have no yard use a planter instead.

The important thing is not exactly how you use your St. Joseph, says Sister Clare Stephen of Pauline Books and Media, but to honor him.

The prayer

First, it must be said, that being Catholic is not a prerequisite; anyone with faith can ask St. Joseph for help.

Once the little guy is deposited into the dirt, say a few words over him. The online shop stjosephstatue.com suggests a prayer that starts this way: "Remember, O most chaste Spouse of the Virgin Mary, that never was it known that anyone who implored your help and sought your intercession was left unassisted."

Or you can be more direct: "St. Joseph, guardian of household needs, we bury you now to help us in the sale of our property."

Or make something up, something respectful, for the faithless or superstitious will not benefit, Realtor Cheryll Woods-Flowers says.

The need

Phil Cates, the operator of stjosephstatue.com, has been selling kits since 1990. His enterprise, based in Modesto, Calif., went virtual in 1996.

He says sales have increased each year.

"But then it really started exploding when the real estate market heated up in 2000," Cates says.

Sellers hoped St. Joseph would bring them bigger profits, he says. One apartment in New York City fetched $800,000 more than the asking price.

And, apparently, the helpful saint doesn't limit himself to homes.

"We've had people who've sold their boats and motor homes," he says.

If sales exploded in 2000, there was something akin to the big bang in 2005, just as residential real estate markets began to soften, Cates says. Sales became especially brisk along the two coasts and in Arizona, Nevada and South Florida.

Cates, who is also a mortgage broker, says investors hoping to flip properties had been fueling the real estate boom to that point, making up about 25 percent of the market.

Typically, speculative buyers make up less than 10 percent of the market.

During the past two years, Cates has sold "tens of thousands" of his St. Joseph kits at $9.95 a pop. If his sales keep up this pace, he says, he might give up his day job.

The 'hysteria'

"Bad news always fuels some hysteria," says Bill Harrison, a lecturer on real estate finance at the University of South Carolina and president of the Charleston-based Harrison Company. But the real estate market churns in cycles, and every so often there's going to be a downturn.

"There are a whole lot of people in their 30s and 40s who have never seen the tail end of a real estate cycle," Harrison says. "We haven't had a true real estate recession for 15 years."

When you're not familiar with how the market works, you're more prone to panic, he says.

Thus St. Joe.

But Harrison calls the current downturn a healthy correction and not something to worry about. Not yet, anyway.

Home values have depreciated as much as 13 percent in some places, but considering the historic run-up in prices since 2000, that's no surprise, he says. What's more, most areas in the country haven't even lost the equivalent of one year's appreciation. Home prices still are higher than they were two or three years ago.

While it might have taken just weeks to sell a house in 2004, now it takes a few months. But a six-month inventory is still pretty healthy, he says. It's when one year or more is needed to sell that builders and brokers have reason to worry: They're missing out on an entire calendar cycle.

Harrison said downturns in the real estate market invariably provoke an overreaction among sellers, which, in turn, fuels the downturn. The important thing is to stay cool, he says.

And trust St. Joe.

The effect

Woods-Flowers, a full-service broker based in Mount Pleasant, says she's seen a slowdown. Her sales are off about 18 percent from last year. But, she says, buyers sense the opportunity — prices are falling, interest rates are still pretty low and inventory is plentiful — and sales activity actually increased in November and early December, usually a slow period, she says.

Maybe that's because of St. Joe.

Woods-Flowers, who is Catholic, sheepishly sought out St. Joseph last year, worried that the practice of burying the figurine was somehow sacrilegious, but the nuns at Pauline Books reassured her. One of them saw the Realtor's badge and asked, "Are you looking for the St. Joseph statue?"

Woods-Flowers bought five.

On three occasions, the broker performed the ritual without the sellers' knowledge, she says. Sometimes the homeowner is happy to go along.

"No, do it, whatever, fine, go ahead," one told her, eager to unload the property.

The practice didn't seem strange to Woods-Flowers. She remembers how her grandmother would appeal to another saint — St. Anthony, patron saint of, among many things, lost items — when she misplaced her keys.

The agent

At Pauline Books, Sister Clare says the Daughters of St. Paul don't advocate the use of St. Joseph for commercial purposes, but they don't object to selling the figurine so long as the customer is well-intentioned.

"You receive according to your faith," she says.

The fact that some make the effort to find St. Joseph at all seems to imply a degree of faith — enough, Sister Clare says, to satisfy the nuns.

The little book of novenas to St. Joseph is available separately.

At the beginning of October, the sisters ordered 200 statuettes. Normally, it would take a good four months to move them all, Sister Deborah Marie says. They were gone by the end of that month.

It seems every third customer is looking for the sacred agent, Sister Clare says.

"When someone comes in asking for St. Joseph, I usually ask, 'Suitable for burying?' "

The sale

Dean Tokarsky, a real estate agent for Southern Homes in Goose Creek, recently helped Yana and Lenny Draves sell their Mount Pleasant home. Tokarsky wasn't surprised when Yana Draves asked him about the practice of burying St. Joseph.

"Have you heard of it?" she said.

"Yes, I have heard of it," he answered.

So the agent provided her with a kit he ordered online.

The Draveses listed their home the last weekend of May. At the end of July or beginning of August, Yana buried her statuette. At the end of October, a contract was signed, and on Nov. 20, they closed.

"It didn't hurt anything, and it worked," Yana said. "You never know. I guess it's a matter of faith."

She says she followed the instructions that came with the kit, more or less. Her "For Sale" sign had shifted a bit in the dirt, leaving a space into which she could slide St. Joseph, feet up, facing the road.

By the time the house sold, the Draveses had moved out and, swept up in the turmoil of transition, Yana didn't go back to retrieve her saint.

"You're supposed to dig it up, but I didn't," she says. "I'm not Catholic."

But she mentioned it to the new owners at the closing. They didn't flinch, she says.

God knows if St. Joseph is still buried there.

Sunset

The decline of Southern rural Jewish communities

It's a serene and lovely place where hundreds of Sumter's Jews are buried. A certain vibrancy buzzes in the warm air, for this burial ground is visibly active with use. People come and go, leave their stone markers and flowers, keep the car path that circumnavigates the gracious gazebo green-free.

Anita Rosenberg, visiting the town she spent half her childhood in, stops by the grave of her parents, Herbert and Virginia Rosefield, to pay her respects and remember the time when this city's sole synagogue, Temple Sinai, was a thriving centerpiece of Jewish life, rich with tradition and history, filled with families and literally glowing with the light that filtered into the sanctuary through magnificent stained-glass windows.

Few people today are left to marvel at that warm light. Either they are buried in the cemetery or they have left this rural corner of South Carolina to pursue careers and raise families elsewhere. The congregation has dwindled to a handful of elderly worshippers, and the fate of Temple Sinai is sealed. It will close soon.

The full-time rabbis are all gone. The Sunday school is no more. There will be no new generation to carry on. The people in Charleston — at the Reform synagogue Kahal Kadosh Beth Elohim and at the Jewish Federation — will act as executors of Temple Sinai's estate. In the months to come, they will figure out what to do when the last observant Jew utters the last prayer and conjures the last memory in the old building. They will ensure that the comforts and grace of the centuries-old cemetery do not abandon the dead.

They will do so because of strong bonds between the two communities that date to the inception of the Colonies. They will do so because Southern Jewish life transcends any specific place.

Other Jewish communities — in Kingstree, Aiken, Orangeburg, Georgetown and Walterboro — have seen similar declines, even as Jewish populations in larger cities such as Charleston, Greenville and Columbia have grown.

All of these smaller rural communities in South Carolina and beyond share a similar story: A thriving merchant and professional class, with origins among the earliest Jewish settlers, provided plenty of reason for the sons to follow in their fathers' footsteps. They inherited the trades, shops and professional careers practiced by the older generation. And they invited other Jews, new immigrants and extended family members living up North, to join in the bounty.

When towns grew, opportunities arose, and Jews were among those to seize them, often invited in to help bolster the urban business and professional classes. By the time World War II ended, Jewish populations in the state's larger cities and towns were booming (relatively), and synagogues were teeming with worshippers, according to historian Dale Rosengarten, curator of the Jewish Heritage Collection at the College of Charleston.

While the rise of the Jewish community in small towns across the state was noteworthy, it was a phenomenon not unique to South Carolina, Rosengarten said. "It was national, it may not even have been regional," she said.

Sumter

In Sumter, a commercial crossroads, the postwar years were characterized by strong textile, manufacturing, biotech, retail and medical sectors.

Starting in the 18th century, the city drew many Jews from Charleston; the two communities are strongly connected even today.

Rosenberg's grandfather had located there from Charleston to start a men's hosiery mill. And she spent many of her earliest years attending services at Sumter's Temple Sinai, where her father served as cantor.

Robert Moses, 91, remembers when the synagogue had a youth group, religious school and full-time rabbi. Its members were active in the city's civic life. Moses, who worked in real estate, was president of the Rotary Club. One of the temple's rabbis served as president of the

YMCA. Moses' brother, Richard P. Moses, was mayor of the town in the 1970s. His uncle, Herbert Moses, sat on City Council.

He said Sumter's residents always have welcomed Jews, and intermarriage was common. "They loved us to death," Moses quipped.

Roger Ackerman, 80, moved from a small town in North Carolina to Sumter with his family in 1965. Temple Sinai still was enjoying its postwar peak. Jewish families from nearby towns such as Summerton, Bishopville, Kingstree and Manning streamed into Sumter for weekend services, Ackerman said.

Perhaps 200 families once gathered at the synagogue then. Today, about 40 members are left, and most are in their 80s or 90s, the two men said.

Moses married a Catholic woman with whom he had five daughters. Three moved out of state; one lives in Charleston; the youngest, Elizabeth, is the only one who converted to Judaism. She was active in revitalizing Georgetown's Jewish congregation, which has benefited from snowbirds and the tourist industry, and now works as a state park trooper in Union.

The decline of Sumter's Jewish community can be attributed partially to the ease with which everyone got along, Moses said. "Jews were well-accepted by non-Jews, so assimilation was rampant," he said.

Exacerbating the situation were rabbis who threw the baby out with the bath water, he added. They would not marry interfaith couples. They would deny non-Jews formal roles and responsibilities at the synagogue. "They turned their back on them."

Ackerman has three children, all of whom have moved away. For a congregation to survive, someone must be there to receive the flame. "You've got to have young people," he said.

A few years ago, those who remained at Temple Sinai began to discuss its imminent fate. It was a difficult topic, Moses and Ackerman said.

"This whole process is a very emotional thing for all of our members," and especially for those who were born in Sumter, Ackerman said. "The congregation deserves a lot of credit. Some small congregations refuse to face reality."

They already had been saving money, so they set up two endowments, managed by the Coastal Community Foundation, one for KKBE's use with regard to the building, and one for the Charleston Jewish Federation, which will maintain the cemetery in perpetuity.

The Temple Sinai congregation contacted David Sarnat, then president of the Atlanta Jewish Federation and now president of the Jewish Community Legacy Project, to help them create something like a living will. Rosenberg, vice president of administration at KKBE, is acting as the Charleston-Sumter liaison.

For now, the synagogue will continue to operate — and prepare for the end.

"At what point do you say the temple is finished?" Moses asked.

Walterboro

The same dilemma is playing out in Walterboro, where 91-year-old Bernard Warshaw presides as patriarch of Temple Mount Sinai, the small synagogue near the center of town.

At its postwar peak, the Jewish population in Walterboro reached about 35 families. They would meet at the Masonic Hall to pray. In the late 1940s, it was decided that the community needed a synagogue, and in 1951 the cornerstone of Temple Mount Sinai was laid.

"We had a vibrant little temple," said Warshaw's wife, Ann. "We had a sisterhood, Seders, holiday celebrations."

Today, average attendance at a lay service is five. The temple seats about 100.

Warshaw, who attended The Citadel in Charleston with Robert Moses, joined the service and saw intense action in the European Theater. He fought his way up the Italian peninsula, participated in the Battle of the Bulge and eventually penetrated deep into Germany, reaching the Dachau concentration camp eight hours after it was liberated by the Americans. He opened two of the ovens himself. And he took a number of photographs of the bodies.

Remarkably, he emerged from the war physically unscathed, and in 1945 he joined the family business — Warshaw's of Walterboro — a clothing store. The store was started by his parents, Murray and Dotty, 25 years earlier when they purchased it from Philip Bogoslow, and they maintained strong business ties to Charleston.

"Henry Berlin (the Charleston clothier) used to call us his country store," Bernard Warshaw said.

On Jan. 1, 2000, when Warshaw was 80, he closed the store and retired from the clothing retail business. None of the Warshaws' three daughters live in Walterboro, and only one lives nearby in Charleston.

At a recent Friday evening service, as a thunderstorm burst in the sky, Lewis Harris led prayers with his wife, Warshaw, the Siegel family and a couple of others in attendance. Afterward, Paul Siegel recalled when there were three or four Sunday school classes, when traveling rabbis cycled through Walterboro, when visitors appeared regularly in the pews.

The last big event was Joseph Siegel's April 2010 bar mitzvah. Joseph traveled to KKBE for his Hebrew lessons.

Paul's wife, Jayne Siegel, who was raised Methodist and who participates in both faith traditions, noted that synagogue membership isn't the only one to decline in recent decades. Small-town churches, too, have seen congregations dwindle as people move away.

For now, the doors of the little temple will remain open. Walterboro's Jews are not ready to face the problem their brothers and sisters in Sumter are dealing with, Warshaw said.

A robust and charismatic presence in the community, he is the force around which the town's few remaining Jews gather, and he is not ready to let this distinctive social and religious component of Walterboro, this history that continues to be made, slip from his grasp.

"We (give) a lot of credit to Bernard Warshaw, not just here, but all around the state," Paul Siegel said, for he is a primary source of Jewish pride and identity. "We are as strong as we believe."

Sunset

At Temple Sinai in Sumter, Moses and Ackerman cope with a combination of worry and peace. They know their beloved synagogue is in good hands, that KKBE will consider carefully the options and do the right thing.

But they know that none of the options are ideal: Perhaps the building will be sold to a church congregation. Perhaps it can be protected by the city or state as a historic site. Perhaps it will become a Jewish museum.

"We are deathly afraid it will be torn down," Moses said.

Its 11 stained-glass windows, made in Germany more than 100 years ago, are magnificent testaments to what once was a flourishing community. Each is dedicated to a founding family — Schwartz, Levi, Moise, D'Ancona, Moses, Ryttenberg and others — names recognized by most of the town.

At the cemetery, the warm sun emphasizes the storm clouds accumulating to the south. Rosenberg leaves the grave of her parents knowing she will have many opportunities to return.

Too often, aging religious communities fail to make the necessary provisions to safeguard their property and history, said Judi Corsaro, chief executive of the Jewish Federation of Charleston. But Ackerman and Moses and the rest of Sumter's practicing Jews are visionaries. "They made some really hard decisions for their community," Corsaro said.

Those buried in the graveyard, and those to die in the years to come, will have a secure resting place.

"It's comforting to know that such an important cemetery, or burial ground, where your relatives are laid to rest, will always be taken care of," Corsaro said. "We feel like it's a privilege to be a part of this."

Magic ... or Mystery?

Supernatural more than good vs. evil

Is Harry Potter evil?

Goose Creek resident James Hartnett thinks so. Hartnett, 72, is a concerned grandfather who says that, with the recent release of the final "Harry Potter" book and the latest "Harry Potter" movie, he's worried that what he perceives to be the anti-Christian nature of the popular franchise will poison the minds of the young and susceptible.

"Churches should take a stance against 'Harry Potter,'" he says. "Children should avoid ungodly things, (and) we have a big responsibility in shaping the minds of children."

J.K. Rowling's "Harry Potter" stories, enchanting to hundreds of millions of fans, feature sorcery and the occult and contain no overt Christian elements, Hartnett and other critics say. Good and evil are blurred, they say, and the supernatural is disassociated from God and his kingdom.

"Sorcerers" surely will be sent to hell upon their death, according to Revelation 21:8. "Idolatry and witchcraft" are sinful, according to Galatians 5:20. And magic is broadly condemned in Deuteronomy 18:10-11, which reads: "Let no one be found among you who sacrifices his son or daughter in the fire, who practices divination or sorcery, interprets omens, engages in witchcraft, or casts spells, or who is a medium or spiritist or who consults the dead."

A world in which magic is used to achieve ends that have little to do with Christian salvation, therefore, is idolatrous and an abomination that should be avoided, many Christians argue.

The Rev. Cress Darwin, pastor of Charleston's Second Presbyterian Church, says it might be a matter of semantics, but he embraces the mysteries of his faith, rejecting the idea that magic is part of it.

"I'm very comfortable with the mysteries of life and the mysteries of God," he said. "They are purposeful for our good and efficacious for our wholeness."

While many Christians believe that all magic is inherently bad, some scholars say that magic also can be good. Defined as a harnessing of a supernatural force to influence or change events, objects, people and physical phenomena, magic was once an integral part of most religious practice, and in some cases still is, says College of Charleston religion professor June McDaniel. Whether it's good or evil depends on one's point of view.

"When it's 'our' magic, we call it a miracle; when it's 'their' magic, we call it evil," McDaniel says.

Supernatural practices

Virtually all magic originates with indigenous cultures and their shamans who, through various means, regularly accessed the metaphysical realm and acted as an intermediary between members of the tribe and the gods, scholars say. This critical role, duplicated in numerous ways by spiritual practitioners throughout the centuries, never has been abandoned. All religions, whether institutionalized, tribal or personal, rely on some form of communication with the divine.

Until the 16th century and the advent of Protestantism in Europe, people tended to conceive of existence in terms of three essential realms, McDaniel says. These were the earthly (mankind and nature), the divine (God and heaven) and the supernatural (spirits, angels, saints, demons and souls, existing in either an ethereal or netherworld).

The latter, supernatural dominion is accessible to humans in the earthly realm and, in fact, enables them to reach the divine, McDaniel says. It was often in this intermediary cosmos that man and God mystically interacted, learning from one another.

To penetrate the supernatural realm and to achieve new understanding, humans have relied on several methods: tarot, hermetics, alchemy, astrology, altered or ecstatic states, ritual healing and mysticism.

Lee Irwin, chairman of the religion department at the College of Charleston and a teacher of religious esoterica, names three basic kinds of magic: the black art, in which demons are invoked for evil purposes; natural, which typically combines certain physical elements, then imbues the combination with supernatural power through ritual; and angelic, which seeks divine intervention from heavenly beings.

In each case, amulets or charms are worn or used in rites to produce a miraculous effect. For example, practitioners of solar healing might combine sundry yellow objects, such as jewels, sunflowers, saffron or other herbs and golden wine.

"You bring these things together in correspondence and create a ritual, and you get a very positive effect," Irwin says. You harness the healing force of the sun. The sun does in fact have healing powers: It helps our bodies produce vitamin D; it warms us when we are cold. It does not require much generosity to appreciate how some believe the sun can also benefit mind and spirit.

Many rituals involve the use of music, Irwin says. Even in the Christian tradition, communal music in the form of hymn singing helps to evoke a spiritual aura, he says.

"Angel magic" in Western cultures typically involves invoking archangels (Michael, Gabriel or Raphael), angels or saints, but doing so carries some risk, he says.

"How do you know it's an angel and not a demon?" Irwin asks. The person calling for intercession must discriminate between good and evil.

Christians today tend to consider such practices sinful and dangerous, Irwin says. Theologically, magic is profoundly threatening, for "the invocation of powers other than God seems to undermine God's authority," he says.

"As soon as you bring in angels, you can't help but bring in demons," he adds. "To avoid being fooled by a demon in the guise of an angel, you stay away from them."

Bert Keller, pastor at Circular Congregational Church and former professor of ethics at the Medical University, says the traditional conception of magic holds that magicians learned the technology that enabled them to manipulate the invisible world. People believed they could harness forces far more powerful than the merely physical.

Sorcerers, driven by ego, practiced personal magic. They used technology — roots, herbs, plants, energies, light, smoke and other materials — to access the supernatural, he says.

But the most harmful kind of "magic" is a dark force called shadow magic, he says. It resides, in part, in humankind's collective unconscious, some believe, and is brought forth to do evil. It's the kind that possibly has contributed to the terrible genocides and wars in history, Keller says, the force that consumes the unthinking mind and easily seduces.

Jewish mysticism

To understand their place in the world, primitive cultures practiced animism, a belief that souls inhabit all objects. It also attributes personified souls to animals. These tribal cultures devised complex mythologies in which a human's life-spirit interacted with various supernatural forces, according to Nevill Drury, a scholar of the occult.

The first monotheistic religion, Judaism, discarded such practices in favor of a single, all-powerful God, who perhaps could best be understood through a mystical use of words, for words themselves held the secrets of the sublime and the force of the divine, notes Rabbi Achiya Delouya.

Delouya, principal of Addlestone Hebrew Academy, says the Jewish faith consists of two main schools of thought: the rational school whose proponent is the medieval Jewish philosopher Moses Maimonides, and the esoteric school, which explains the human experience in mystical terms.

The teachings of kabbalah, which originated at Creation and are manifested in part in the Hebrew Bible, rely on numerology and the power of letters to reveal truth. Kabbalah offers complex explanations about the nature of God, the construct of the human soul and reasons for evil in the world. The word itself means "to receive."

"Kabbalah deals with the internal part of what we do," Delouya says, "that which animates us." And it must be understood in the context of the Jewish concept of Tikkun Olam, mending the world.

When God created the universe, the light illuminating the world was so vast and powerful it could not be contained by man's Earth and shattered into millions of shards. It is this imperfect universe that mankind inherited, and it is for the Jews to repair it by reclaiming these broken shards of light through prayer and the performing of good deeds, Delouya says.

Kabbalah helps Jews recognize their essence and their function on Earth, he adds. It provides the tools to crack the code of Creation:

Hebrew letters, each a creative entity with a corresponding number, sound, color and gender, as well as philosophical interpretation. Kabbalah is a portal to a supernatural world where truth is revealed.

Supernatural examples

Judaism is informed by an oral tradition of folklore and academic study, as well as written Scripture. The Hebrew Bible is full of episodes in which God and man use supernatural force, often to destroy.

The stories of the great Flood, Joseph's experience in Egypt, the destruction of Sodom and Gomorrah and the life of Saul and Samuel contain examples of the supernatural, but it is the story of Moses and the Exodus that best demonstrates how God's "magic" is more powerful than man's, McDaniel says.

In Pharoah's court, God transforms Aaron's staff into a snake. Pharoah's sorcerers do the same, but then Aaron's snake-staff swallows the Egyptians', symbolizing the strength of God's Chosen People.

Then follows a series of supernatural phenomena, 10 horrific plagues: blood, frogs, gnats, flies, death to livestock, boils, hail, locusts, darkness and, finally, the killing of the Egyptians' first-born sons. While fleeing Egypt, Moses invokes the power of God to part the Red Sea.

"Moses is the archetypal figure for magicians in the Judeo-Christian tradition," McDaniel says. He could exercise such power and wield such influence because he knew to harness the "right" kind of supernatural force, she says. "It was a matter of the right God versus the wrong God."

The New Testament, especially the Gospels, contains many examples of supernatural power. Its primary practitioner is Jesus Christ, who performs numerous miracles, from healing the sick and disabled to exorcising demons, walking on water and multiplying a few loaves of bread and some fish into enough food to feed 5,000 people.

The Gospels' telling of mystical transformations also demonstrates Christ's power over all realms. In the mountaintop Transfiguration, for example, the figures of Moses and Elijah appear alongside a glorified Christ, striking awe and terror into the hearts of his disciples.

According to the Bible, the Resurrection, which shows how flesh can transcend the earthly realm to enter the realm of the divine, demonstrates Christ's supernatural omnipotence.

In the Catholic Mass, the Eucharist celebration includes a transformation of bread and wine into the flesh and blood of Christ, a process called transubstantiation. Catholics believe that in changing the substance of the sacraments, Christ's soul and divinity are made present, according to Catholic doctrine.

These examples are some of the well-accepted mysterious events and practices of mainstream Christianity. But the faith has seen its share of mystics who have mostly remained on the margins over the centuries. The New Testament Apocrypha, including the Gnostic gospels, while not part of the official Christian canon, has inspired arcane practices, including esoteric cosmology and ethics, according to McDaniel.

Hermeticism, a set of philosophical and religious beliefs originally set forth by the Egyptian Hermes Trismegistus, led to the development of the Rosicrucian movement in the 15th century, which combined mysticism with Christian tradition. Rosicrucians relied on alchemy and divine magic to repair vices and defects of the soul, and, in essence, as a universal cure.

Today, Catholics appeal to saints, Sufi practitioners dance, meditate and read poetry in their quest for divine unity, Jews decipher the numeric symbolism of their Hebrew letters and some Protestants speak in tongues, exorcise demons and heal the sick and disabled through the laying on of hands and invocation of God's grace.

Everyday magic or mysticism

Perhaps the most common method of invoking the supernatural is simple prayer. Believers ask God or Jesus Christ or the saints or angels to intercede in earthly affairs, to influence outcomes, grant wishes and offer protection and oversight. Sometimes prayers are offered before sacred relics — a lock of hair, a tooth, a bone from a saint — for it is thought that such objects wield supernatural powers, that they are still imbued with some soul force, according to religious doctrine.

Jose Mayen says he believes in the supernatural as a force that comes from God. A parishioner at Immaculate Conception Catholic Church in Goose Creek, Mayen says the saints and the dead intercede in the lives of believers through prayer and ritual all the time, though the miracles expressed by them originate with God.

"People who have died are praying for us, are helping us," he says.

Some, including College of Charleston's Irwin, suggest that consciousness itself — thinking — is magical. Irwin points to meditation and dream states as examples. Dreams are rational ways to access the subtle and sublime, he says. They are our mind's way of working out the issues of the day and conflicts of the past, often using a space that's neither earthly nor divine but somewhere in between.

Many people experience flying dreams in which they are projected into a world where nature and supernature are in harmony, Irwin says. In this often vivid, multidimensional place, spirit and matter are part of a single whole, a realm in which the dreamer expresses himself magically, and sometimes achieves new levels of understanding or awareness, Irwin says.

Most monotheistic people, however, have learned to dismiss or marginalize the supernatural, relegate magical experience to the dust bin of a sinful occult past, Irwin says. But this repression of the sublime, he says, saps the human experience of some of its vitality.

It used to be that humankind relied on that intermediate supernatural realm all the time, McDaniel says. This was the pathway to the divine.

"Now, the only way to access the divine is to die," and wait for the resurrection of the body and life everlasting, she says.

There is no talk of a Christian divine in "Harry Potter." No resurrection of the body. No everlasting life. Just boys and girls learning their craft from wizards and witches, facing challenges and obstacles, and coming to understand the power of love.

So is Harry Potter evil?

Darwin, pastor of Second Presbyterian Church, says it's just entertainment and doesn't trouble him in the least. In fact, he likes the moral themes in the series, the good-versus-evil formula and the ultimate defeat of the dark forces. Christians confident in their faith need not fear a little fantasy, he says.

"We are the believers of the mysteries of God," he says. "Things happen all the time in people's lives that are miracles. ... I am changed by prayer. Is that magic or is it a mystery?"

Drawing the Line

Mixing faith with politics raises questions

The phrase "separation of church and state" appears nowhere in the Constitution. That was among Thomas Jefferson's contributions, and it's a modified version of the expression he included in an 1802 letter to the Danbury Baptists in Connecticut. His actual phrase is: "a wall of separation between Church and State."

What the First Amendment of the Constitution does say is twofold: That government shall establish no official religion and that everyone is free to worship (or not worship) as he sees fit.

That, you might think, leaves a bit of wiggle room. But in the intervening years since the Bill of Rights was ratified in 1791, numerous Supreme Court decisions, rulings almost as powerful and binding as the language of the Constitution itself, have left considerably less room for interpretation. Thanks to these rulings and to the original establishment and free exercise clauses of the First Amendment, those who practice a religion in the United States are free to believe whatever they want.

But to protect the rights of all, the faithful are not free to do whatever they want.

They cannot impose their beliefs on others. They cannot allow public institutions to endorse one form of faith over another. The reason: to guarantee freedom for all.

So the line between church and state is clearly drawn. It separates the public and private realms. It allows all kinds of belief but prevents one from becoming "official."

So why all the fuss? Why the debates about prayer and science and abortion and euthanasia and stem-cell research and prayer in schools and the display of religious symbols and same-sex marriage and school vouchers and faith-based initiatives and family values?

Nonbelievers don't mind that the public sphere is kept secular, but some among the religious have argued that the establishment clause unfairly mandates religious indifference, while the free-expression clause is implicitly burdened with artificial conditions. Sure, you can express your religion freely — if you stay at home or in church — but caution to those doing it in the name of government.

In truth, compromises have been made. Currency includes the motto, "In God We Trust." Public meetings at all levels of government often begin with a prayer or invocation, and, since 1954, the Pledge of Allegiance contains the phrase, "one nation, under God." The courts have not objected to what they consider "ceremonial deism." But how much is too much?

Some stats

More than three-quarters of Americans call themselves Christians, according to an August 2006 survey by the Pew Forum on Religion & Public Life. The survey found that many Americans are ambivalent about the mix of religion and politics, 69 percent say liberals have gone too far in keeping religion out of schools and government, while 49 percent complain that Christian conservatives have gone too far in trying to impose their values on the country.

Nearly one-quarter of Americans were classified by the survey as white evangelical Christians with conservative political attitudes. More — 32 percent — were identified as "liberal or progressive Christians."

Six of every 10 white evangelical Protestants and 32 percent of all Americans say the Bible's authority outweighs the will of the people, according to the survey.

A significant majority of white evangelicals — 62 percent — say the Bible is the actual word of God and should be taken literally. But 65 percent of Americans generally subscribe to the view that the Bible is meant to be interpreted. About 67 percent of Americans say they consider the United States a Christian nation, survey results state. (By contrast, 60 percent thought so 10 years ago, according to the survey.)

Hot issues

Last month at a Darwin Week forum, College of Charleston biology professor Rob Dillon gave a slide-show presentation explaining the evolution of the intelligent design concept and describing in some detail why he believes religion and science cannot co-exist in the same classroom.

It's not that creationism cannot be discussed in schools, he said, it's just that it should be confined to religion or philosophy classes. Science, after all, depends on quantifiable data and hypotheses that can be tested, he said. It's about devising sound theories that, because of the exhaustive research required to establish them, come as close as anything to empirical fact.

As for God, he added, why would anyone want to prove his existence? Religion is a matter of faith.

After the presentation, a College of Charleston biology student stood up to assert a different view: Creationism, she said, ought to be included in the science classroom so students can weigh its merits against those of science and decide independently which they prefer.

Last November, when voters in South Carolina and seven other states were deciding whether to support a ban on gay unions, Charleston attorney Susan Dunn made a distinction between the civil and religious conception of marriage.

For civil society, she said, marriage — any kind of legal union — is a good thing. It obligates individuals to support one another, relieving the state of that burden. Marriage, therefore, is one of the institutions we use to stitch together the fabric of society, she said. It's part of the social safety net.

Those who oppose gay marriage do so mostly on religious grounds, Dunn said. But should certain religious values determine how a fundamentally civil institution is defined?

In the provocative documentary film "Jesus Camp," which was nominated for an Academy Award this year, evangelical Christian children are seen protesting abortion during a trip to Washington, D.C. Standing before the Supreme Court, the children and their adult chaperons seal their mouths shut with pieces of thick red tape that have the word "LIFE" printed on them. Later, Kids in Ministry International Director Becky Fischer addresses them: "You made a covenant with God tonight, that you're going to pray to end abortion in America. Don't take that lightly. Don't be a promise-breaker. Be a historymaker."

Most people can be found somewhere between the extremes, notes the Rev. Monty Knight, pastor of First Christian Church in West Ashley and president of the Charleston chapter of Americans United for Separation of Church and State. It's possible to be morally opposed to abortion yet pro-choice at the same time, he said. The moral repugnance someone might have toward abortion does not mean another's rights should be curbed, he said.

Chad Brand, professor of Christian theology at the Southern Baptist Theological Seminary, said the court's incremental expansion of the establishment clause over the years has impinged on the free-exercise clause.

For example, it was appropriate for the Supreme Court in Engel v. Vitale (1962) to strike down a New York Board of Regents policy on teacher-led prayer in public schools, Brand said. But prohibiting prayers before a football game or preventing a small prayer group to assemble at school is going too far.

Law and revelation

The problem is that some among the faithful are not always allowed to choose how they practice their faith, Brand said.

American Indians in Oregon were prohibited by a 1990 Supreme Court decision from using peyote during worship ceremonies, he noted. In that case, controlled-substance laws trumped the free-exercise clause of the First Amendment (however, Catholics were permitted to use wine during Prohibition 60 years earlier).

And then there's "natural law," an ethical theory concerning how nature intended things to be, and "general revelation," a theological term that refers to the universal aspect of God.

It's obvious that a butcher's scale ought to be accurate, Brand said. It's obvious that a man and a woman ought to join together in marriage. There is "complementarity" between the genders.

To argue that the state should not have something to say about marriage or sexual relations is hypocritical, he said. Laws exist preventing incest, for example.

Abortion, too, is subject to natural law or general revelation, he said. It makes little sense to terminate a pregnancy when life is apparent. An ultrasound at five weeks often will reveal a beating heart.

John Simpkins, professor of constitutional law at the Charleston School of Law, said the Supreme Court, despite a recent shift rightward, has proceeded with caution even as Congress has attempted to promote certain "religious freedoms" advocated by Christian groups.

It could be that a group of Christian athletes is prevented from meeting at a public school after hours because school officials don't want to be liable for breaching the establishment clause, Simpkins said. Or because officials don't want to open the flood gates, suddenly endorsing all expressions of religion on school property. Yet prayer in public can be OK so long as it's not led by an official, and there is no threat of coercion, he said.

The 'wall' made man

The Rev. Barry Lynn, national director of Americans United for Separation of Church and State, said the fight persists, but that those trying to insert Christian doctrine into U.S. politics, while influential, have not gained in numbers since the politicization of the evangelical movement in the 1970s. Children of the religious right are not growing up to be as conservative as their parents, he said.

"They're reacting to the world as it is and not to the world as some would have them believe it is," Lynn said.

In the last election, conservative Christians lost a stem-cell research vote in Missouri, an abortion vote in South Dakota and a same-sex marriage vote in Arizona, he notes. And the intelligent design argument suffered a big blow with the Kitzmiller v. Dover Area School District case in Pennsylvania during late 2005. In its wake, creationists on the Ohio and Kansas school boards were voted off.

But the core of the conservative movement still is fueled by a powerful religious fervor, he said.

"You can easily mistake a temporary setback for a permanent change in attitude," Lynn said.

Unlike some progressive Christian thinkers, such as Jim Wallis and Tony Campolo, Lynn does not believe the conservative tide is turning and has hunkered down for the long battle.

Though Christians in America "have a dizzying level of freedom," he said, they nevertheless claim to be victimized, restricted from expressing their religious beliefs.

"When I've asked how they are persecuted, they say, 'Well, I couldn't put up a Nativity scene in a firehouse,'" Lynn said.

Knight said it's imperative for him to remain vigilant. Americans are too easily distracted by a "culture of entertainment" and materialism and not willing enough to engage in serious debate over important issues, he said. At church, it's no better.

"We're held hostage by niceness," he said. "The point is not to offend others."

But argument is needed because keeping church and state separate is essential for the well-being of both, Knight said.

"Anytime you have a state church, religious vitality is diminished," he said. "Secular government enhances religious vitality."

Take Italy. Catholicism is ubiquitous. Portraits of the "Madonna and Child" decorate the halls of nearly every public building. Crosses are mounted above hospital beds. National holidays are dictated by the church calendar. Yet most Italians are unperturbed, indifferent to the public displays, Knight said.

When religion is mandated, it loses its sting, he said.

"Christianity is an innately free religion, not something that's coerced," Knight said. "By its nature, it's a choice."

Waiting for Salvation

Believers at Overcomer commune abide controversial leader

C ANADYS — Their prophet speaks.

"I am the sign! Can I say that? I have faith enough to believe it."

Brother Stair is the Last Day Prophet of God.

Brother Stair is a sinner.

"I'll tell you what happened! I committed adultery with two women here! And I went to the people and apologized."

That was nearly six years ago. About 40 members of this reclusive Christian commune just north of Walterboro lost faith in their prophet and left. Accusations were flung about. Charges were filed. The authorities swooped in. Ralph G. Stair, then 68, was arrested and jailed for 77 days, eventually pleading guilty to two reduced charges of assault and battery.

His loyal followers at Overcomer Ministry farm and his radio listeners around the world were bereft.

But some continued to walk with Stair, and in the years since 2002, the community has tried to regain its footing.

Today, about 70, including nine children, live in this secluded place, growing their own food, making their own clothes and worshipping together on Saturdays in the Tabernacle. Residents include people of all ages, black and white. Self-sufficient, they survive by faith and hard work, even under the glare of scrutiny.

Their self-imposed exile, odd ways and controversial leader who preaches that the end of the world is upon us have fueled the flame of public concern and prompted numerous investigations by law enforcement officials at taxpayers' expense.

Who, exactly, are these reclusive end-of-times Christian farmers?

The commune, tucked in this corner of rural South Carolina just beneath Interstate 95 in Colleton County, is austere, featuring few amenities. Mobile homes and handmade houses provide nominal shelter from the elements. Rows of clotheslines extend from the laundry room. A refectory offers space for communal meals.

In an adjacent kitchen — well-equipped with a refrigerator, cupboards, food counters, a large cast-iron oven and stove top pieced together by the residents, mixing tools and other accoutrements — several women prepare the large daily meal.

The Overcomer community is both a place of its time and a place that functions oddly outside of time.

"This is the LAST generation!" Stair has exclaimed, his words posted on the Overcomer Web site. "THIS is the generation that God is going to POUR out His Wrath upon. I'm telling you that Christ IS coming! ... We haven't got any time Left."

And so the 20-year-old community is rooted in the present, ever on the lookout for the Messiah, ready for the imminent ecstasy of salvation.

Yet this is a farm like so many others that have been organized throughout history. It is an assembly of people who, for various reasons, have mostly removed themselves from the world, even if the world has a tendency to burst in on them unannounced and uninvited, resident Joseph Cline explains.

"When you have a great light, you draw a lot of bugs," Cline says. The great light is Brother Stair and his message of doom.

The message is everything

Aside from Jesus Christ and the promise of the Second Coming, the radio operation at Overcomer farm is everything. The agrarian life this community has embraced serves to support the broadcasts. Brother Stair spends hours at a time, whenever the spirit moves him, riffing on apocalyptic themes, the dissolution of the world's great political powers and the miracle promised by Christ's return.

Residents take a vow of poverty, giving their material wealth to the commune. A dress code requires modest attire, just as the Bible instructs. Men wear long pants and shirts with collars; women wear long skirts that cover their legs.

The priorities are the work and the Word.

"We don't put too much stock in worldly things," Cline says. "So we don't put too much money in them."

Cline, a former rock-'n'-roll musician, may be the only resident here with air conditioning, perhaps because his home is nearest to the gate and Cline tends to serve as the community receptionist. Another resident jokingly refers to Cline's modest home as Overcomer's Taj Mahal.

The day begins before sunrise. The farming is done during early morning hours. The planting, irrigation, harvesting or upkeep are usually finished by 9 or 10 a.m.

The crops are plentiful and include okra, peppers, cucumbers, garlic, onions, eggplant, spinach, carrots, pumpkin, broccoli, chard, collard greens, tomatoes, peanuts, watermelon, cane sugar, bananas, blueberries, grapes and various citrus. The excess is sold at a shed by Augusta Highway.

In the midst of the blueberry patch, a pole rises toward the heavens. A speaker is mounted at the top, and Brother Stair's aging tenor voice rings out. The speaker serves two functions, Cline says. It allows men and women in the fields to listen to the message, and it enables them to monitor the radio signal. Should the speaker go silent, it means the words of the prophet die at his microphone.

Stair spends hours at a time in the studio. Even his preaching in the tabernacle is sent out to the world beyond. The church and the radio studio are solar-powered. Just beyond a hand-dug, rainwater-filled ditch euphemistically called the "Long Pond" lies the photovoltaic panels — eight of them, each with six segments capturing sunlight and storing the energy in an impressive battery array housed in a nearby structure.

Harnessing the sun in this way ensures that pumps will always run to irrigate the crops and that Stair's voice will never be silenced in the event of a standard power failure.

In the event of such a failure, Cline's computer might shut down, the lights would go dark, the laundry machines would stop working, but through it all, the prophet would keep preaching.

Mark Hodgson, 25, and Dave Mull, 46, are the technicians who keep the broadcast going.

In a small equipment-filled building near the Long Pond, Hodgson, who has lived here for more than six years, says the broadcast is delivered to Pittsburgh by a satellite uplink. From there, it's transmitted to

25 stations throughout the United States and to Israel. Shortwave radio enables listeners in Germany, Slovakia and the Czech Republic to hear Brother Stair.

A decade ago, Brother Stair could be heard on 120 stations, Hodgson says. Overcomer Ministries has collected letters of support from people in 192 countries, he says, and many of them include financial contributions. The commune receives thousands of letters a year.

In a good month, its collections can reach $100,000, money used to pay for annual expenditures of about $1 million, according to Stair. In recent years, the farm has failed to break even, spending more to sustain the operation than it takes in from loyal listeners.

Mull says he's been a follower of Brother Stair since 1996. The commune has been his home for 3 1/2 years.

"I'm a believer in what he preaches," Mull says. "The world is in such bad shape right now."

In the quiet of a recent humid morning, Christopher Landry, the resident horticulturist and self-proclaimed Overcomer "fanatic," describes his journey from Texas A&M University, from which he graduated with a degree in economics, to the Christian farm in Colleton County.

Landry worked on a ranch while he was still in Texas, learning about plants and greenhouse operations. Then he worked at a publishing house in Dallas that required his presence on Saturday, the traditional Sabbath day, a day of rest he preferred to observe but couldn't.

In 1983, he was saved. It wasn't a particularly dramatic event, Landry says, more like a conviction affirmed.

"No one had to beat me over the head to believe the Bible. I took it literally and easily, but didn't know how to live by it."

One day, an acquaintance who was a Seventh-day Adventist asked Landry if she could find a job at the publishing company, and he warned her about the requirement to work on the Sabbath.

"God said (to me), 'Did you hear your own words?' That day I tendered my resignation."

Landry had heard Brother Stair on shortwave radio in Medina, Texas, a tiny crossroads town of a few hundred people.

"Everything he preached I already believed," he says. "I saw an opportunity to practice my faith in an environment that's not antagonistic to it. ... I believe Western civilization is going down the tubes. I'm a risk-averse person; I like to get out of the way when the fist is coming."

The troubles

Many outsiders don't think well of the Overcomer farm, authorities say. They think the people who live there are a bunch of religious zealots. They think members of the community are part of a cult whose leader has brainwashed his followers. They think Brother Stair is a white supremacist, a pervert, an extortionist. They think he runs a slave-labor camp.

The authorities — the State Law Enforcement Division, Colleton County Sheriff's Office and county coroner — have raided the farm several times, sometimes in the middle of the night, Stair and other residents say.

Sometimes the visits are prompted by disgruntled former residents who claim they were abused or exploited, Stair says. But no one is a captive here; anyone unhappy with the lifestyle can leave. And this has happened, Stair says. He even has returned some money to those who decide, sometimes after years on the farm, to abandon the prophet and his message.

He doesn't want trouble.

But in August 2001, Brother Stair made "an involuntary and partial disclosure regarding sexual battery against several young adult women who were 'Stair believers,' " according to a SLED case file. Stair says he apologized to the community for two adulterous affairs.

SLED's criminal case against Stair lists several accusations, including criminal sexual conduct, breach of trust and unlawful burial. The case file reveals that former members of the community accused Stair of intimidation and financial wrongdoing.

Last July, after he pleaded guilty to two reduced charges of simple assault and battery, the case was closed, according to SLED. He was sentenced to time served. Now, a civil case is pending.

Stair and his supporters say many of the allegations have come from people who found the going too tough at the farm and saw an opportunity to take advantage of someone easy to demonize.

The first of the troubles came shortly after Stair established Over-comer Ministry in the late 1980s. A stillbirth prompted an investigation then, too, though no charges were filed. The baby, three weeks overdue and 11 pounds, failed to get enough oxygen during a prolonged birth and suffocated, according to news reports.

No doctor was involved in the birth. The residents of the farm say they distrust and shun doctors. They attribute illness and death to God's will.

In December 1993, another child died several weeks after its birth, but the death was not reported to authorities, according to the SLED investigation. A search warrant was secured for the purpose of locating the grave and exhuming the body for an autopsy.

Then, a little more than a year ago, another stillbirth. On the gnat-ridden path between the fellowship hall and laundry room, Broth-er Stair points to the house where it happened.

The father was a trained medic. But the baby's grandmother was unhappy, according to Stair and Cline. She called the authorities and tried to get her daughter to seek medical attention.

"(Sheriff's deputies) would come out in the middle of the night de-manding to see the mother and verify whether she was still alive, caus-ing no small amount of stress," Cline wrote in an e-mail.

Eventually, the mother went to the hospital for a C-section, but it was too late, Cline wrote.

The county coroner automatically orders an autopsy of anyone who dies at Overcomer farm.

Daily bread

In the kitchen, a group of women prepare for the day's big 3 p.m. meal. Cline's wife, Cyndie, is making the bean cakes and eggplant-tomato sal-ad. A row of fresh, whole-grain bread sits on a ledge.

The community, which raises a few goats and cattle, makes its own cheese, mayonnaise, butter, cottage cheese and sour cream.

Breakfast is served at 7:30 a.m. after work in the fields is well under way. School starts after breakfast, and the community-taught children get a break at noon and finish before dinner. Leftovers from the big meal are made available after the evening prayer for those still hungry.

While the men mostly perform the hard labor and the women mostly do domestic chores, the community is not averse to employing people according to their particular skills, Landry says.

"We promote the biblical roles of men and women," he says.

Rebecca Hodgson, 22, is Mark Hodgson's wife. She is helping 6-year-old Natasha Leer make sour cream. Natasha, sitting at a counter, turns the contents round and round in the bowl.

Rebecca Hodgson says she has been visiting Overcomer farm since 2002 and got married this past May. She says she's used to the Christian environment and rural lifestyle; it's how she grew up. When she was 15, she tried to kill herself, she says. Her father heard Stair on the radio and that gave him an idea: perhaps Rebecca would benefit from the ascetic life of the commune.

On the radio

The gnats swirl around Brother Stair's neck. He is tall and wiry, donning a thick white beard. His speech is high-pitched and direct. He is sure of his message but occasionally will rely on a follower to identify the specific passage of Scripture he alludes to.

"If somebody wants to know how to make it right with God, I'll show him," Stair says.

Repent. Change your ways.

Brother Stair is a marathon preacher. He can spend hours in the solar-powered broadcast studio without food or drink. He gets carried away; he loses track of time. His record is 11 hours at one sitting.

He is not interested in proselytizing, he says. It's not converts he seeks but, rather, faithful Christians who are not yet aware that the Apocalypse has begun to cast its shadow over the ends of the Earth, he says.

Brother Stair is adept at manipulating the technology. He adjusts the 16-track mixing board, logs on to the instant-messaging feature on the computer, opens his oversized Bible to the Book of Revelation and ensures the telephone answering system is functional. Multivitamins are stacked on a nearby table. A bottle of Fixodent sits to one side.

He is railing against corruption, society's dependency on the almighty dollar. He is predicting the imminent end of times, for once the world's two superpowers crumble, so shall man's reign on Earth. He is preaching about the glory that accompanies Christ's coming. The Soviet Union fell apart in 1989. Now the United States is compromised, its borders permeable, its influence diminished, its markets globalized.

And religion is susceptible to global markets, too, the nondenominational prophet says. Institutional religion is corrupt. It provokes Armageddon.

"That's why they hate us out there! We don't buy and sell. ... Love of money is the root of all evil, not fornication."

And that allusion to his own sins puts him on the defensive.

"I confessed my sin, never justified it," he says. "The Lord said to me, 'You're dealing with a generation of immorality, and you are not different than anyone else.'"

Then he turns to the computer and exchanges a quick greeting with a faraway listener, first asking for his identity. Some messages come from pranksters, or worse, he explains, so Brother Stair always dips a toe in the water before taking the plunge.

The reply comes. It is from a true follower, Brother Stair decides, then types "God bless you friend."

"There is nothing more confusing and more complex than religion," Brother Stair says. "The end is coming, and the only future you have is in Christ."

Members of this community firmly believe that future can be secured here, in the fields, under the hot sun, fending for themselves, putting their trust in the Lord and supporting their prophet as he sends out his message across the airwaves.

"This," Brother Stair says, "is the good life."

Women in Religion

Art exhibit challenges inequity and exclusion
in church traditions

Blame Eve.

Before monotheism — before God the Father created man in his image, then woman from Adam's rib; before his favored kings of Israel married their multiple wives to secure their dynasties; before Christ appointed 12 men as his Apostles — ancient gods and goddesses mingled as equals, more or less, provoking, protecting or frustrating humankind, and blurring the line between flesh and spirit.

Everything had its gender. The Earth was female. The Sun was male. And every object had its associated gendered god. It was difficult to distinguish between the object and the idea of the object, so most ancient cultures didn't bother to try. Poseidon and the ocean's waves were one.

All deities had their specialized power. Each served its purpose. And men and women paid tribute.

When the Kingdom of Israel emerged, slowly over centuries, polytheism gave way to monolatry (the worship of one favored god without rejecting the existence of other gods) and, later, Hebrew monotheism.

Yahweh clearly preferred to dote on men. When he looked down at his creation and saw that it wasn't very good after all, he assigned the patriarch Noah to the task of saving the world's beasts from deluge and beginning humanity anew, according to Torah. God blessed Noah and his sons.

When God wanted to test Abraham's faith, he ordered the patriarch to slay his firstborn son, Isaac. Meanwhile, Abraham pretended his wife, Sarah, was his sister and offered her up to the pharaoh in exchange for favor and wealth.

When it came time to rescue the Hebrews from slavery in Egypt and grant them autonomous nationhood, God called Moses.

Meanwhile, women were designated as second-class citizens, to put it politely. They could not wander about in public without their father or husband. They could not talk or reveal themselves to strangers. They could not testify in court. They could not complain when their men married other women, but they were put to death should they commit adultery, or be suspected of doing so, or fail to prove unequivocally their virginity before marriage. They could not complain (to men) when raped. They were owned as property. They were ruled over by men.

Many point to the Creation story as the first reason why women were the ones to get short shrift. Eve was Adam's "helper," made from Adam's flesh. Her weakness prompted her to pluck the forbidden fruit, thus causing the fall of humankind, the original sin that thereafter separated man from God.

It was her fault.

* * *

Today, though, Americans live in a society that abides (or tries to abide) by democratic principles, including the equality of all people regardless of gender, race, age, sexual orientation and income. Everyone has a shot at success, we're told.

Yet many religions continue to lag behind secular society, says artist Fletcher Crossman, who long has contemplated the idea of gender inequality in church, determined to represent that idea in paint. Religions point to Scripture and tradition to justify such inequality, claiming that since God has deemed it so, there's really nothing that can be done about it, he said.

But Crossman, seven other artists and a local pastor disagree.

They are mounting an exhibit at the Circular Congregational Church, 150 Meeting St., called "She Shall Be Called Woman" that explores the feminine in religion. The free show opens to the public at 6:30 p.m. Saturday and runs through Sept. 11. The church will be open most days.

Its centerpiece is Crossman's "Apple Thief," a 15-by-12-foot, four-canvas composite of a crucified woman. The painting certainly challenges traditional conceptions of Eve and Jesus, but it also succeeds in reinforcing at least one traditional theological view: That through Christ's sacrifice, Christians are redeemed from original sin.

There are lots of things God ordained or sanctioned once upon a time that we deem outrageous and unjustifiable today, such as genocide, rape, war, slavery and human sacrifice, Crossman said. That's the reason for the show: to get viewers to question long-held beliefs and consider their origins, to contemplate the ever-changing status quo and to imagine a more inclusive theology.

For the Rev. Bert Keller, pastor of Circular, the show is an affirmation of the values promoted by the congregation.

"It fits broadly into the basic commitments of the church," he said. "That would include equality and empowerment."

Women, Keller pointed out, form the core of religious faith. They are more spiritual than men, are more affiliated with a specific church than men, attend church more often than men, pray more than men and believe in God more absolutely than men, according to the Pew Forum on Religion and Public Life. They are a significant majority in all Christian traditions, according to Pew data. (In Judaism, Islam, Buddhism and Hinduism, men are the active majority.)

Yet "religious traditions have shamed and abused and discriminated against women in unconscionable ways," Keller said.

The church has reinforced double standards, persecuted women suspected of witchcraft and denied women full participation, he said. Some discrimination continues today. Even liberal congregations often don't value the role of women sufficiently, Keller said.

So when Crossman approached him with the idea for an exhibit that explores these ideas, Keller was delighted, he said.

The other local artists displaying their work are Virginia Derryberry, Julie Jacobson, Sharon Lacey, Max Miller, Lisa Shimko, Carl Turner and Peggy Howe.

Junius Wright is the show's curator. A teacher of European literature at Academic Magnet High School, Wright likes to integrate visual arts in the classroom, using literary analysis to study paintings and other works of visual art, he said.

He will bring his 10th-grade students to see the show so they can consider the art alongside books such as John Milton's "Paradise Lost" and other titles that have female protagonists, he said.

Wright, who worked with Crossman on a 2008 installation at the Gaillard Municipal Auditorium, is updating the new show's Web site with artist interviews and other content "to extend the experience beyond the show" itself, he said.

* * *

Crossman said he scrutinized many crucifixion paintings in preparation for his own. In the studio, he worked with model Abbi Miller and photographer Jack Alterman to create a series of sketches and referential images, settling ultimately on chains, not nails, and a fully clothed figure. He said he wanted to avoid the use of blood, expressions of agony and any visual innuendo that might be interpreted as sexual.

He wanted the figure to be recognizable, modern and expressionless. Her calm gaze hints at accusation, not because of any emotion the figure projects, but because of the preconceptions and attitudes of the viewer, he said.

Influenced by Salvador Dali and Caravaggio, among others, he created a picture that uses space and perspective in ways that are not typical of most crucifixion imagery. Looking at it, the viewer is at once forced to contemplate both the Christian idea of salvation and the role of women in the church, Crossman said.

Louise Doire, a religion instructor at the College of Charleston who teaches a course called Religion and Feminism, said women's exclusion from leadership and ministerial roles is an unfortunate historical fact that has been justified in different ways over the centuries.

In the first of the two Creation stories, Adam and Eve are made by God simultaneously: "male and female he created them." In the second Creation story, Eve is made of Adam to be a helper. She partakes of the fruit from the tree in the midst of the garden because "she saw that the tree was good for food, and that it was pleasant to the eyes, and a tree to be desired to make one wise" — all good and benign reasons, Doire said. Yet God is angered nonetheless because his warning went unheeded and so punishes the couple with mortality, pain, labor and shame.

Might this destiny have been meted out no matter what? Is it possible that Adam and Eve were set up? Is it fair to blame Eve for their fall from grace?

"Hebrew Bible scholars have attempted to convince me that there is nothing misogynist about the Creation story," Doire said, "that there are no inherent claims to women's inferiority in the story itself. What happens subsequently is, Eve becomes a prototype of all women. And her inferiority and subjugation are justified by the story through her having been created second, by a different method than Adam and for a particular purpose" — to serve the man.

Religions historically have justified their doctrines and actions by citing these early Bible verses, Doire said. Women were viewed as child-bearers obligated to remain obedient to their men.

But Jesus adopted a different approach. He forgave women rather than condemning them. He embraced them as friends and disciples. He invited them to join his ministry and travels. He honored them as capable individuals of value. In so doing, he upended the traditional view of women. Some scholars argue that Mary Magdalene was not only a beloved confidant of Jesus, but a co-leader of the Jesus movement, Doire said.

Paul the disciple, too, named women as apostles, deacons, prophets and teachers. In early Christianity, Doire said, "Women had prominent roles in household churches. Many of these were led or funded by women."

Since the earliest Christians believed Jesus' second coming was imminent, there was a sense of urgency and so no real need to establish long-term institutions, Doire said. But when, decades later, Jesus was nowhere to be seen, institutions began to be formed within the Roman Empire.

"The Christianities that were going to survive were the ones that modeled themselves after Greco-Roman hierarchies and organizations," she said.

And those organizations were patriarchal.

College of Charleston religion professor June McDaniel said that, according to St. Augustine, the church's ecclesiastical structure on Earth is meant to reflect the supposed hierarchy of heaven. The pope, bishops and priests mirror the sacred rule of God, the archangels and angels,

McDaniel said.

It's based on revelation, she said.

"People follow revelation. If revelation says that there's a male hierarchy (in heaven), then that's what you want to have on Earth. This is the issue known as hermeneutics, or interpretation. How do we understand revelation? Do we take it literally or symbolically?"

In the early church, McDaniel said, during the patristic period (first three centuries), there were four levels of Scriptural interpretation: literal, ethical, allegorical and mystical.

Literalists believed the Bible was a historical document.

A moral view advanced the idea that the Bible contained teaching stories that helped people understand how they should behave.

The allegorical approach held that characters in the Bible represented virtues and vices (the serpent signified temptation; Eve represented corrupted innocence).

The mystical approach held that everything in the Bible represents part of a complex relationship between the human soul and God.

"In the early church, most educated elders (bishops) who were most respected had many interpretations," McDaniel said. "If we look at the Bible as having many levels of meaning, if it is a complex document, then we can understand the role of women in different ways."

In recent decades, religion increasingly has found ways to better accommodate women, said Stephanie Hunt, who chairs the Community Advisory Board of the Women's and Gender Studies Program at the College of Charleston.

"It's changing because women and men have recognized the incredible spiritual gifts that women bring to the church and beyond," Hunt said.

Older generations can struggle to reimagine traditional roles and question the rationale for male authority in the church, she said. But art shows such as Circular's can prompt people to consider the contributions of women.

"God's bounty is deep and rich, and women are there, and need to be there," she said.

Ultimate Gift

Brother Edward prepares for a new beginning — death — with a joyful heart

H e has been reading Psalm 73 from the Athanasian Grail Psalter lately, moved by its closing lines.

You will guide me by your counsel and so you will lead me to glory.
What else have I in heaven but you? Apart from you I want nothing on earth.
My body and my heart faint for joy; God is my possession forever.
All those who abandon you shall perish; you will destroy all those who are faithless.
To be near God is my happiness. I have made the Lord God my refuge. I will
tell of your works at the gates of the city of Zion.

These words of Asaph speak to him. Asaph is envious of the foolish and wicked, the ungodly who prosper in life and do not endure suffering but rather inflict it; he is envious until he enters the sanctuary of God where divine destiny is inscribed.

I was stupid and did not understand, no better than a beast in your sight.

Brother Edward Shivell reads aloud these verses and his voice wavers. It is the bliss of death.

His arrival at this threshold was achieved in a typical way — cancer — but his path was uncommon, lined with purpose, poverty, obedience, chastity and an unceasing quest to embody goodness.

His departure originated in a smoke-filled pub his father owned in Wilkes-Barre, Pa., a bar called Shivell's Tavern frequented by coal miners after each day's hard work. His father liked to raise a glass with his customers. When his father died years later, in 1959, Brother Edward was sequestered and unable to attend the funeral, for the life of a Cistercian monk is austere and unhindered.

Before his submersion in the monastic life, with its six ritual Hours and daily Mass, its silence and manual labor, its commitment to the elements of Earth and concentration on the "now"; before he was merely a monk, he was merely a boy growing up in church, attending Catholic schools and avoiding college, for which he had no patience.

Brother Edward sometimes lacks patience. Always he has been focused on the moment, on his place in time, on his shifting proximity to the divine; always he has strived to move closer, closer, so that he might experience his ecstasy. He is 80. He has been waiting a long time.

"Where was I in the beginning? In God," he says. "There is no past, no future in God; there is always now."

Yet there is life, its physical reality. There are senses and perceptions. There is food to prepare. There is chicken manure to clean up, mushrooms to grow. God is ever-present but separate. God is mysterious. And Brother Edward is not whole while he walks and thinks and works. But he is closing in, he is closing in.

"That's what makes it so exciting," he says. "You're going back to where you were." Reunion.

* * *

Shivell joined the Navy in 1948 after high school and spent four years aboard the destroyer Compton, working in the supply office.

"I liked it, I liked it very much," he says. "I goofed around, kind of nicely."

He would look out at the sea, its waves shimmering silver in the moonlight, and contemplate the beauty of creation. "I liked to be aboard the ship at night. It was the silence and solitude that really grabbed me."

He wrote a letter to his pastor: Perhaps he was meant for a vocational life? He had planted the thought in his priest's mind, where it lay like a dormant seed as he finished his tour of duty.

After the Navy, Shivell wanted to avoid his pastor. He knew a visit would shine like sunlight on that seed and prompt it to sprout. He did not know whether he was certain of his thoughts, whether he ought to fuel the fledgling leaf.

But this is how God works.

The priest arranged for Shivell to visit a group of Franciscan friars in Scranton, Pa. It was the end of July 1952. He signed up that afternoon and began his Novitiate on Aug. 15, traveling to Lake Geneva, Wis., where he spent three months on retreat.

Franciscans are active monks. Their mission requires them to serve the poor and disadvantaged. They venture forth often into the secular world. During the Lake Geneva retreat, Shivell met two men from the Trappist Abbey of Gethsemani in Kentucky. They were contemplative monks of the Cistercian order, and they carried with them a booklet describing the simple and silent life at Gethsemani in words and photographs.

A Cistercian monk is concerned only with two forms of work: liturgical and manual. Staring at the photographs in the booklet, Shivell envisioned his future.

* * *

Mary said, "You see before you the Lord's servant, let it happen to me as you have said." And the angel left her.

Let it be done. After a joyous communal Thanksgiving, Brother Edward left the Franciscans and moved to Kentucky. His parents were distressed. Franciscans were fine, but Trappists? Memento mori, memento mori — remember death — these monks intoned constantly, when silence was not enforced. He was permitted to write four letters home each year and to receive four letters each year. What kind of life is this?

But they visited their son in his new home and saw that he was happy.

Brother Edward had two choices: to become a choir monk and priest or to become a contemplative brother and laborer. The abbot thought he should study for the choir and sent Brother Edward to Newton, N.J., to learn Latin and the ways of priestly leadership. After one semester of training, the young novice, who had refused college and preferred quiet manual labor to scholarly exercise, returned to Gethsemani and became a silent monk.

He was more than two years at the Abbey of Gethsemani, learning, obedient, contemplative. In South Carolina, a monastic "foundation" had been established by the Kentucky monks in 1949. It was dependent on its Mother House to the north. It housed two dozen brothers, many of whom were novices.

Some of the young monks had left, but seven others came to the foundation in Berkeley County in 1951. "The Seven Gifts" they were called. Four years later, the foundation became an independent abbey, and it needed more manpower and an administration of its own.

The Cellarer of Gethsemani, who is the monastic official in charge of provisions and business enterprise, agreed to oversee the new abbey, called at the time "Immaculate Heart of Mary" and "Our Lady of Mepkin," on the condition that he could bring 10 others with him.

Brother Edward had been consecrated into the monastic life under the title "Immaculate Heart of Mary." God's mysterious plan was briefly glimpsed. He volunteered to go.

* * *

And so Brother Edward was among the first monks to take up residence at the new abbey. Today, three other founding monks — Brothers Gregory, Joseph and Robert — remain active members of the community.

During the first decade, the monastery upheld a strict code of silence, fasting and frugality. The brothers remained separate from the priests of the choir. Novices remained separate from those who were professed.

Choir members had two slices of bread and a quart of coffee for breakfast; brothers were permitted five slices of bread and coffee because they performed physical work. No one ate meat.

The Second Vatican Council (1962-65) resulted in a loosening of the rules. Many brothers left, novices arrived. Limited verbal communication was allowed in designated areas. Those pursuing higher studies could leave the abbey for periods of time. The monks could visit family at home, attend funerals.

An abbey must support itself. Enterprise at Mepkin during those early years included a bakery operation (cinnamon rolls and bread), pasturing cows for milk and meat, a lumber business and cultivation of camellias and azaleas. Later, the monks would manage thousands of egg-laying hens and experiment with gourmet mushrooms.

Brother Edward cut down trees for a while, then he worked in the nursery and in the kitchen. He has labored with his fellow brothers for 55 years. He has known four abbots. He has witnessed the quiet transformation of Mepkin Abbey, the force of hurricanes, the construction of new buildings, the growing engagement with the land both on and off the property, the development of various lines of business.

In 1984, he took a leave of absence to be with his mother, who was dying of cancer. One of his two brothers died of cancer. His two sisters died of cancer. Now he is dying of cancer.

* * *

Diagnosed with prostate cancer in 2003, Brother Edward underwent 42 radiation treatments. He seemed to respond well, though images of his bones (where prostate cancer often spreads) failed to appease his doctors: titanium in his hip joints, the result of earlier hip-replacement surgery, caused a bright flash to obscure part of the images.

Prostate cancer thrives on testosterone, so patients often are subjected to a drug called Lupron, a luteinizing hormone-releasing agonist that shuts down the body's production of testosterone and, thereby, starves cancer cells.

But it has side effects. Brother Edward suffered from severe hot flashes. "I didn't like it," he says. "There is no quality of life. I was just miserable all the time."

He quit the drug in 2006. His PSA level went from 20 to 957 over the course of a year and a half. His cancer spread. His bones began to ache.

But it turned out the cancer had not spread to his bones; it was arthritis that had taken root there. The cancer was invading his lymph nodes, from head to foot.

He endures some discomfort but remains an active participant in the life of the monastery. "Jesus accepted suffering; I can tolerate pain," he says.

He is trying to understand Jesus Christ, who was happy to be loved, who sought out affection and who received it from Mary Magdalene.

"I'm being touched the same way he was touched with manifestations of love," Brother Edward says.

When he dies, the brothers will anoint the body as Mary Magdalene wished to anoint Christ in his sepulcher.

But his spirit already will be mingling with the divine.

* * *

What no eye has seen and no ear has heard, what the mind of man cannot visualise; all that God has prepared for those who love him.

Death is a door opened by God. The door is reached after a million small steps. The passage instills a radical joy; oneness is its reward.

Every night before going to sleep, for 55 years, Brother Edward has prayed for a restful night and a peaceful death. He says the prayer out loud.

"God must be kind of tired of hearing this," he jokes.

He is thinking of the funeral rites, of the community of Mepkin Abbey monks that will gather soon and anoint his body with holy oil and say the prayer of healing, the same prayer intoned over someone ill or in need of surgery.

He is remembering the funerals he has attended, the procession into church, the tolling bells, the way the body is laid out, clad in a monk's robe, the constant praying, the always-present monk, the Mass and burial service.

He is speaking of his fellow monks who know him and love him and understand him. He is thinking of the journey he has made and of the journey to come.

It is so simple. The Earth is both womb and final embrace. The dying soon know perfection after an imperfect life, after this sojourn abounding in mystery.

"I don't fear dying, I look forward to it," Brother Edward says, struggling to express his inexpressible joy. "I'm going to God, who is absolutely tremendous."

And death, should it come during this season of renewal, will be his Christmas gift to treasure.

Brother Edward is thinking of these things and smiling.

Richard Hagerty's 'Way of the Cross' a Meditation on Suffering and Search for Truth

H e knew he would do this eventually: paint the Stations of the Cross. After he retired in 2016, at age 65, from the Medical University Hospital as a distinguished member of the plastic surgery team, Richard "Duke" Hagerty dove in, recalling his childhood and conjuring all that he learned in the Far East. It took more than four years to complete the "Via Crucis" cycle, which hangs inside Circular Congregational Church's bright Lance Hall through May 12.

Fourteen surrealist images, 3 feet by 2 feet and framed by Robert Newton with wood that mimics the cross, portray the arrest and torture of Jesus, his long plod to Golgotha, his crucifixion and deposition, and his ascension to Heaven. The paintings, a meditation on universal suffering, are arranged so viewers can view them in succession or simply stand contemplatively in the middle of the space.

Hagerty also created a bold "Last Supper" featuring Apostles with abstracted expressions and the central figure of Jesus, robed, blue-faced, staring out at the viewer.

In his work, one detects elements of Pablo Picasso and Jean Miro, of Hieronymus Bosch, of Salvador Dali. His version of surrealism might be labeled "sophisticated Naive art," for Hagerty is entirely self-taught, yet he makes vivid work of intricate detail imbued with symbolism and poetry. It conveys an ever-growing accumulation of experiences and ideas informed by his travels; his interest in Buddhism, mysticism and other forms of spiritual exploration; his active dream life; and a unique view of the world.

In his most fruitful artistic moments, Hagerty thinks of himself as a conduit who paints more with his brain than with his hands.

"The secret and the joy of real creativity is learning when and how to get out of the way and let the process take over," he said. "Then it becomes bigger than yourself, and then not yourself."

For a while he quit signing his pictures. Too much ego involved, he thought. But his wife, writer and poet Barbara Hagerty, thought that omitting a signature might make selling the paintings a bit troublesome. So Duke figured he'd put his dyslexia to good use and sign them backwards.

When he retired from medicine, he was wary of the human tendency to avoid severing all ties to something one loves. Surgery defined him for decades. Hagerty became known for his charitable work around the world fixing cleft palates and other deformities. And his travels introduced him to other cultures. He was fascinated by Southeast Asia and became a student of Buddhism, thanks in part to a beloved interpreter, Mito, with whom he always worked when visiting Vietnam.

So to quash temptation, Hagerty tore up his medical card, "like Cortés in Mexico burning all the ships so nobody could get back," he said.

The "Via Crucis" ("Way of the Cross") was his first big project after he retired from his day job.

"I have always wanted to do the Stations of the Cross," he said. "I was raised Catholic and always intrigued by the pageantry and mysticism."

Each lifespan includes a certain number of moments impressed so forcefully upon one's consciousness they leave a lasting mark. One such moment for Hagerty was Good Friday at St. Mary's Church when he was perhaps 12 years old. Morning light streamed through the windows into the sanctuary, illuminating the smoke from burning incense. The procession featured colorful costumes, capturing the imagination of the young boy.

It was an experience imbued with grace and flair, stimulating Hagerty's nascent aesthetic, emotional and spiritual sensibilities. And it represented safety from the difficult world outside, where his severe dyslexia made his school days nearly impossible to endure.

The tortoise

Another moment impressed in his memory: Hagerty was in Vietnam around 1990 to teach local doctors how to perform corrective surgery for cleft palates when Mito took him to visit an old monastery surrounded by a dry moat at the bottom of which lumbered an enormous old tortoise.

The monk accompanying them pointed to Hagerty, then pointed to the tortoise, his gestures clearer than any words could be: "You are the tortoise."

Hagerty understood instantly. Like the giant creature below, confined to a mote that limited its view, Hagerty was similarly inexperienced yet able with time to discern that much lay beyond that which his senses could perceive.

And so he studied Buddhism, began practicing meditation, explored the science of the mind, learned about Carl Jung and his theories of synchronicity, universal archetypes and the collective unconscious. He scrutinized figures in mythology and folklore, such as the birdman and bull; he mined the Bible and contemplated its stories; he delved into numerology seeking connections to the divine; and he stared in the face of contemporary crisis — environmental degradation, political turmoil — so he might find sources of inspiration for his dynamic "paintings of the mind."

He was the tortoise, stretching his neck, seeking answers, answers that led to more questions.

When it came time to paint the Stations of the Cross, he began with a storyboard and a color wheel, sketching his compositional and figural ideas across long sheets of paper. And he contemplated the meaning of sacrifice and suffering, the various roles of women, and the ways Eastern and Western thought intersect.

"It was so intense!" he said. "A psychological minefield."

The instinct

To escape the explosive terrain, Hagerty retreated to family and friends. He sought intellectual exercise with Gary Smith, a magazine writer and Charleston resident who, using a different set of tools, delves just as deeply into the human psyche.

They met in 1986, when Smith needed a bit of melanoma removed, discovered they shared an interest in excavating truth, and decided to play tennis together. After a year or two of athletic fraternizing, Smith learned that Hagerty was reading Friedrich Nietzsche.

"And I love Nietzsche," he said.

So they started meeting once a week for philosophical conversations.

They would read the same book, mark it up, then discuss it and how it related to their lives.

"That became a long-time practice together," Smith said.

Then, reading about the workings of the mind, they decided to investigate the impacts of meditation, to "turn the lamp inward." One retreat led to another, and another. They talked about how the ideas they explored together found their way into Smith's profiles, and into Hagerty's paintings. They deepened their friendship.

"He's a very instinctive person," Smith said. "He feels things. Even though we do a lot of intellectual spade work, it doesn't come out the end of the paintbrush in any kind of intellectualized way. It comes out through blood and tissue and the strangeness of human mind."

About a decade ago, the two friends decided they would play music together. They taught themselves how to play guitar. They learned some covers, then started writing songs. They formed a band called Post-Life Crisis. Now and again, they get a gig.

The truth

Jeremy Rutledge, pastor of Circular Church, said he was impressed by Hagerty's imaginative work.

"I was immediately drawn to the colors, the tone, and the dream-like effect of the work," he said. "Spending more time with it, symbols emerge, as do memories and questions. In this way, walking through the exhibition is a wonderfully contemplative experience."

Though on view during the Christian season of Lent, the work really is universal, Rutledge observed, encouraging people of all faiths and philosophies to visit the exhibition.

"Duke's art really resonates in our historic space because the space itself is filled with 'memories, dreams, and reflections,' as Jung said. … In religion, we use stories and symbols, music, art, and poetry to express what we cannot ever fully say. I'm grateful to Duke for what his artwork evokes about the human condition."

Hagerty's artwork perhaps is an outward extension of his inward meditation, which requires discipline and concentration, he said.

The subject matter of this series can cause discomfort, but it can also stimulate the imagination, he said.

"The thing I learned through all of this is that I want a personal experience," Hagerty reflected, citing Nietzsche.

"If you want to achieve peace of mind and happiness, have faith," the philosopher wrote. "If you want to be a disciple of truth, then search."

III.

PEOPLE:
Confronting Life

Introduction

by Jennifer Berry Hawes

As a church is not merely a building, a community is not the sum of its structures and landmarks, no matter how fascinating or immaculately restored. Instead, it is a stew of people, diverse and alike, all brined in shared history, no matter how fraught. Perhaps nowhere is this truer than in the Lowcountry, once a stronghold of slavery, now tourist mecca for music, arts, architecture and the most complicated of beauty. Yet, those who call the place home define it, as do those who visit, and those who visit and then wish to call it home. Each leaves footsteps in the detritus of collective memories that has created a unique sense of place, and of home, few being as endlessly fascinating as ours.

In the pages ahead, Adam Parker celebrates a cast of this humankind. His stories of race and war, history and celebrity carry us alongside the footsteps each has left behind — or is still setting down, one step after another, through our pluff mud and the sand. Thanks to Parker's skilled storytelling, we all can break bread with the Lowcountry's most legendary author, dig in the dirt with a war veteran haunted by combat, and admire the remarkable author of "Vibration Cooking or, The Travel Notes of a Geechee Girl."

Parker writes about each of them, and so many others, with empathy and verve. He clearly finds them all hopelessly interesting, and so every detail he notes, every scrap of dialogue he records, every setting he describes lures readers to share in this interest as well. Over the pages to come, he offers intimate portraits of such luminaries as Vertamae Smart-Grosvenor, Pat Conroy and James Campbell. Yet, he also introduces us to two children abandoned in Liberia who "left one world and entered another," that of classical music, a realm in which Parker moves with precision given his own training there. That easy sifting among people of all sorts of backgrounds and experiences allows Parker, and therefore us as well, to journey with them. Come along.

Jennifer Berry Hawes is author of "Grace Will Lead Us Home" and special projects reporter at The Post and Courier.

Vertamae: A Profile

Standing at the window of her bungalow not far from where the Coosawhatchie drains into the Broad River, she contemplates the marsh.

Across the way is Beaufort County. Today, Interstate 95 takes travelers north, but in slavery days, blacks only had the Underground Railroad.

Vertamae Smart-Grosvenor, who lives on a former rice plantation, looks out across the marsh and imagines the workers who once threw down their rice threshers in exhaustion and disgust, escaping their fate with nothing but the tattered clothes on the backs, wading through the creek beds, hiding in the tall grass and praying that what awaited them was a friendly soul who could direct them to a Railroad weigh station.

Grosvenor imagines the spirits of those slaves lingering in the creeks and the path they forged to a better life. The past is the present. The present is ancient. The ancient is always new.

* * *

When she was born at home near Fairfax, S.C, she weighed three pounds and was called Verta Mae Smart. She was a twin, smaller than her brother, but stronger. Her parents Frank and Clara Smart placed her in a shoebox and kept her by the oven. She survived. Her brother did not.

But there was no proof of her birth.

Years later, when she returned to South Carolina and wanted to renew her passport, she contacted the authorities to request a copy of her birth certificate.

"I'm sorry, we have no one with that name on record," the clerk told her.

"You mean I don't exist?" she said.

She does not know her age, at least not with certainty. "It depends on how old I feel when I get up," she says. She knows only the month and day she entered the world: April 4. Ask her for her proper name, she will cite several. Virter. Verta Kali Smart. Mae. Verta Mae. Vertamae. Space Goddess. Obedella.

* * *

Having no birth date has been liberating. In the 1960s and 70s, Grosvenor was living in the East Village of New York City. Part of the city's black intelligentsia, she frequented jazz clubs and acted in the theater.

For a few years she was a Space Goddess in Sun Ra's Solar Myth Science Arkestra. She was tall and thin, elegant and proud. She designed the clothes. She danced and sang. She read his poetry as the cosmic musical philosopher played free improvisation. She invented the "space walk," a precursor to Michael Jackson's moonwalk.

When the band went to the south of France for a jazz festival, it drew attention.

"Where did you find these people?" someone asked the psychedelic Sun Ra.

"I just thought them up," came the reply.

Vertamae Smart-Grosvenor was born without any record of the event, and she was just thought up.

* * *

When she was around 8 years old, her family migrated north, taking their Geechee ways with them. Verta Smart came of age in Philadelphia. As she aged she grew.

Tall and skinny and interested in the theater, she was teased by the other children. She slouched. She mused about being weird and unwanted.

As a teenager, she would hang out at a coffee shop. Someone told her to check out a young woman playing music at a hotel across the street. Nina Simone, not yet famous, was performing at various venues in Philadelphia after the Curtis Institute of Music declined to admit her. Nina Simone and Verta Smart became friends. Many years later, on July 26, 2003, three months after the famed troubadour died, Grosvenor offered a tribute at the memorial service in New York City.

At 18, Verta Smart read about the Beat Generation, about their non-conformist ways, love of literature, embrace of life and determination to explore the world. If she were a "bohemian" she would be accepted, she thought.

So she took a boat to Europe, alone, uncertain what she would find.

* * *

In Paris, the Beats were finding a freedom of the mind they were missing in the U.S. Verta Smart, too, wanted freedom.

She found the Beat Hotel on the Left Bank. She found a colony of expat artists and writers — the Scottish folk singer Alex Campbell, the American writer Jonathan Kozol, the French painter Lucien Fleury. She would marry one of them, the artist Robert Grosvenor.

Photographer Harold Chapman was staying at the rundown hotel at No. 9 Rue Git-le-Coeur. During the late 1950s and early 1960s, he took pictures of Verta Kali Smart and the others, including Allen Ginsberg and Peter Orlovsky, William Burroughs and Gregory Corso.

In Paris, she began to write. She made her own clothes. She prepared simple, delicious meals based on the heritage she kept safe within her.

She found herself.

* * *

After a couple of years, she returned to the U.S. and settled in New York City. Kali was born in 1962; three years later Chandra arrived.

The 1960s was a heady time for Grosvenor. She became active in the theater, realizing a childhood dream, and even made it to Broadway. Verta Smart played Big Pearl in a production of "Mandingo," a play that ran for just eight performances before closing. Dennis Hopper played Hammond Maxwell.

She had studied acting at the Hedgerow Theatre in Philadelphia under Jasper Deeter and now, in New York, getting a chance to apply her skills.

In 1966, Louis Gossett secured a grant from the Office of Equal Opportunity, and a group of actors, including Grosvenor, mounted a series of improvisations in Tompkins Square. Her two daughters, Kali and Chandra ran around the neighborhood rounding up the spectators.

* * *

When she was in New York she frequented the jazz clubs with poet A.B. Spellman. She brushed up on the Black Power movement. She organized dinner parties. She threw a fundraiser fish-fry for SNCC in its waning years.

She met the Bahamian-American actor Calvin Lockhart — "one of the loves of my life." He was handsome, elegant, talented, sociable, temperamental.

He took Grosvenor to meet Muhammad Ali at the boxer's Deer Lake training camp in Pennsylvania. He took her to England so he might appear respectable before the Royal Shakespeare Company, which wanted him to become the first black actor-in-residence.

When Kali was 5, she started writing poems. Three years later, the photographer Joan Halifax decided the poems should be paired with pictures and published. In 1970, Doubleday agreed. Kali's book led the publisher to her mother's work, and that same year, "Vibration Cooking" was released. It made her famous.

By the early 1980s, Grosvenor was living in Washington, D.C., and contributing stories and commentary to National Public Radio. She reported on the threatened Gullah-Geechee communities of the South Carolina and Georgia sea islands. She reported on the cultural significance of food. She reported on the expatriate experiences of African Americans in Paris.

Her stories were gorgeously told, rich in characters and dimension and unlike most of radio's offerings, her colleagues said. Her cooking show "Seasonings" won a James Beard award. Her renown led to a television show, part of The Americas' Family Kitchen series produced in Chicago, called "Vertamae Cooks."

In 1998, the University of New Hampshire granted Grosvenor an honorary doctorate and promised to send her a chair. She assumed they meant some kind of desk ornament. But it was a real chair, displaying an inscription: "Doctor of Humane Letters."

Soon after the chair arrived, her 10-year-old grandson Oscar asked, "Grandma, is there such a thing as inhumane letters?"

* * *

On the occasion of writer James Baldwin's 60th birthday in 1984, Grosvenor arranged an interview. Baldwin told her to meet him at his house on West 71st St. at 2 p.m.

When she arrived, Baldwin was not there. Then she remembered his reputation for being late, sometimes very late. She waited and waited.

That evening, Baldwin's mother Emma prepared the guest room and cooked up something for dinner. Eventually, the writer returned home, wearing white pants and a navy blazer, looking dapper.

"We talked about what we'd talk about the next morning," Grosvenor says.

Three years later, she was an honorary pallbearer at Baldwin's funeral, joining the immense gathering at St. John the Divine Episcopal Cathedral in New York City.

* * *

In the street one day, when the family was living in Washington, D.C., granddaughter Charlotte put Grosvenor on notice.

"See you later in the week," she said. "See you Wednesday."

This took Grosvenor by surprise. "Oh? Why?"

"I signed you up."

Charlotte's 4th grade class was inviting people of interest to visit with students and talk about their lives.

"And Grandma, can you bring a pan of rice?"

So Grosvenor woke up early and prepared a pan of rice, struggling to get the hot dish into a cab and to the school.

The children gobbled it up, listening to Grosvenor explain its African origins and its cultivation along the tidal rivers of South Carolina.

One asked, "Do you know how to make peas and rice?" Another described the rice dish he ate in Jamaica. Another mentioned the rice she ate in the Dominican Republic. They all knew about rice, and Grosvenor was struck by the way different cultures share certain essential elements.

* * *

In late 2009, Grosvenor was socializing with friends when she began to slur her words and lose consciousness.

She was rushed to the hospital where it was discovered she had had an aneurysm in the brain.

She spent two weeks in the hospital after her operation, then more weeks in rehab.

Grandson Oscar jokingly explained the situation this way: "They had to operate on grandma's brain; they took it out, rinsed it off and put it back."

Well, it was something like that, more or less, Grosvenor says, thinking back over her remarkable life.

Ambassadors of Gullah Culture

Ron and Natalie Daise keep up the storytelling

They've been off the island for a while now, but Ron and Natalie Daise bring their Gullah culture with them wherever they go.

Into classrooms and conferences.

Onto the stage.

Onto the canvas.

Into the pages of books.

Into song.

They are humble people, content with singing and painting and telling stories about the noble blacks who enriched the Carolina Lowcountry with their benefactions and with their blood. Call them the Gullah Power Couple and Natalie Daise cringes a little in discomfort.

After all, a number of people have worked hard to draw attention to and celebrate Gullah culture, from Marquetta Goodwine (Queen Quet of the Gullah-Geechee Nation) and painter Jonathan Green to community leader Emory Campbell and filmmaker Julie Dash, whose 1991 feature "Daughters of the Dust" propelled this unique heritage onto the silver screen for millions to see.

But ask someone now in his or her upper 20s or early 30s about the Nickelodeon TV show "Gullah Gullah Island," and you're likely to witness an unusual kind of nostalgia, the recollection of a formative childhood experience.

The children's show aired 1994-98, for four seasons, and more than 750,000 tuned in for each of what amounted to 70 episodes. The Daises held forth as the indulgent parents of two kids (one played by their biological son Simeon, the other by the daughter of neighbors since their real daughter Sara was too shy).

Songs were pre-recorded in New York City; interior scenes were shot at Universal Studios in Orlando, Fla.; and exterior shots were filmed in Beaufort, where the Daises lived for many years.

Today, Ron Daise is vice president for creative education at Brookgreen Gardens and Natalie Daise is concentrating on her oil and acrylic painting. The kids are grown. The couple lives in a quiet neighborhood outside Georgetown and travels to events far and wide to tell stories of Gullah life.

Felt like home

"Painting is the way I tell stories," Natalie Daise said. "Painting happens a lot, painting is kind of crucial to my well-being. It's my primary means of expression and the thing I do most consistently."

She's started a new series called the "Apparition of St. Harriet" featuring the stoic face of Harriet Tubman enveloped by colorful Gullah imagery. The series is inspired by an old movie, "The Song of Bernadette," in which the Virgin Mary appears before a girl in a grotto.

"What if St. Harriet just suddenly appeared," Daise wondered. "She's very present in my life."

Her "Collard Queen" is a magnificent portrait of a woman decorated with the large textured leaves of the Gullah staple, a reference to the life and land of African Americans on the sea islands of the Southeast.

Her paintings include many elements — African iconography, food items, colorful garb, abstract designs, gold or silver or copper leaf and more — that mimic a Byzantine style, but her real focus is on the people she portrays. Though she has no formal training, Daise has an innate ability to paint profoundly expressive faces and to connect posture with feeling. Consequently, she permits the viewer a glimpse of the mind and heart of her subjects.

"The story to me is in the eyes and in the face," she said. "The spirit of the subject sort of comes through in the painting, if I'm lucky."

She's often lucky.

Daise spends a lot of time in her home studio, but she also works a couple times a week at the nearby Rice Museum downtown, offering tours and helping out in the gift shop. Often, she's thrilled to share the history of slavery along the rice coast of the United States, but sometimes she's taken aback by the ignorance she encounters.

On one occasion, a man in his 30s touring the Rice Museum learned of the dangers of rice cultivation and the short life spans of the laborers.

"Why did they do it then?" he wondered aloud, only to be corrected by his wife's forceful whisper: "They were slaves!"

Natalie Daise, born in 1961, was raised in Rochester and Syracuse, NY. When she was 22, her grandmother, a resident of Lady's Island near Beaufort, fell ill, and the family decided that Natalie would go South to help.

Stepping off the Greyhound bus and touching the Lowcountry soil kick-started a strange alchemy. This Yankee from New York State immediately began to transform into a Gullah-Geechee.

"It honestly felt like home," she said.

She moved into a trailer behind Uncle Simeon's and Auntie Dee's house, accustomed herself to the palmetto bugs and many young male cousins, assisted her grandmother and watered her family roots.

Soon she was off to college, first a Seventh-Day Adventist school near Washington, D.C., then Oakwood College in Huntsville, Ala., the University of South Carolina-Beaufort. She thought she should go into medicine or physical therapy; her family insisted she had the brains for it. But then she met Ron Daise.

Taking the stage

The native of St. Helena Island had earned a degree from Hampton University in Virginia and recently published a book: "Reminiscences of Sea Island Heritage." The volume provided a basis for the development of a live presentation that included songs, storytelling, history and more. Natalie joined Ron on stage.

"My husband told me I was a storyteller," she recalled. "I didn't know I was a storyteller."

Ron Daise quickly understood the potential of a team effort.

"Maybe we could be like Ozzie Davis and Ruby Dee," he thought.

Emory Campbell, then director of the Penn Center on St. Helena Island, invited the couple to perform at a gathering of museum professionals in the mid-1980s. They received a standing ovation.

That led to more gigs, but not always enough to pay all the bills. Natalie did some temp work; Ron worked at the Beaufort Gazette for two years (he was the paper's first black reporter), then did some teaching.

But he knew they were onto something. He loved the Georgia Sea Island Singers. He understood the value of sharing his heritage. He could see how cultural presentations such as the one he'd developed present "old information in new ways, and new information as it's discovered."

And his impulse was not to dwell too much on the miseries of slavery and Jim Crow but to emphasize the accomplishments and artistry of Gullah people.

Soon came a lucky break.

On the island

Plans were afoot to make a movie based on a Gloria Naylor novel. Naylor was living in the Beaufort area but her home was largely unfurnished and not ready for distinguished Hollywood guests, actor Lawrence Fishburne and producer Maria Perez.

Natalie Daise came to the rescue, buying furniture and befriending the author of "Mama Day" and "The Women of Brewster Place." Soon the Daises were part of the company, chatting about the prospective movie. Perez mentioned she was pitching ideas to Nickelodeon and had heard that the Daises were good Gullah storytellers. Maybe that would make a good show, she suggested.

Six months later, Perez was back in Beaufort with a film crew, following Natalie (very pregnant with daughter Sara) and Ron Daise around town for a day. The footage, soon back to New York, excited the Nickelodeon people. A show would be developed.

Fracaswell Hyman was hired as head writer for "Gullah Gullah Island," taking cues from the Daises, working in material drawn from their lives. Most of the more than 25 characters were drawn from real life, and most retained their own names on the show. The cast and crew held to an aggressive schedule, shooting parts of two episodes each week.

"They were so easy to work with, all of them," Hyman said. "I had no idea about Gullah culture when I first started on the show, so I learned a lot from Ron and Natalie. I admired their work ethic. ... It was an ideal situation. Not every situation has been that easy and fluid."

Today, young adults sometimes will tell Hyman how much they loved the show.

"It makes me feel good, makes me feel proud," he said.

Teaching history

Herb Frazier, a former journalist who now is public relations and marketing manager at Magnolia Plantation and Gardens, first encountered Daise in 2005 when Frazier was working on a story about Priscilla, a young woman enslaved in Sierra Leone. Daise wrote songs and poetry. The two men met in Freetown, and they've stayed in touch over the years.

"They're multigenerational," Frazier said of the Daises. "My children know them."

His daughter Amanda grew up watching "Gullah Gullah Island." Frazier received his copy of the Gullah-language "De Nyew Testament" from Ron Daise, who delivered it by hand soon after it was published.

Frazier said the Daises' storytelling approach makes Gullah culture accessible.

"They use their art to educate and inform people about the culture," he said. "It's one thing for journalists to write about it and academics to research, but they put it in a way that people can understand and appreciate. They're entertaining."

At Brookgreen Garden, Ron Daise has become essential. Each Wednesday afternoon he offers a presentation to visitors, projecting slides on the screen and speaking with a sing-song cadence about rice and ring shouts and Jubilee and gatherings and language and courage and mettle and skill.

Keep on movin', keep on endurin', keep on livin', cuz we all have a right to the tree of life...

Walking from the Education Center through "The Village," Daise points to a huge cypress trunk, one of thousands enslaved Africans chopped out of the swamp. It took seven years and many deaths to transform a cypress swamp into a rice field.

It's his voice visitors hear on the audio tour. It's his work visitors appreciate when learning about the history of Brookgreen plantation, now the most visited site along the South Carolina coast.

Daise, whose Gullah identity and accent seemed a handicap when he attended Hampton University in the mid-1970s, now rejoices in its fecundity.

Living culture

By the time Wendy Belser came to Bookgreen Gardens in 2011 to become director of philanthropy and membership, Ron Daise was well established there. He had joined the staff in 2004 and quickly implemented cultural programming that broadened the Brookgreen experience for visitors.

Belser saw the husband-and-wife team perform during the historic site's popular holiday presentation Nights of a Thousand Candles.

"The first time I met Ron, he was singing," she recalled. "I thought, 'Oh my goodness, such talented colleagues I'll be working with!' ... He really captivates all the visitors to Brookgreen who come to enjoy those performances."

When Natalie Daise presented her one-woman show "Becoming Harriet Tubman" at Brookgreen, it quickly sold out, Belser said.

"We had to add performances. It was so powerful, it was absolutely stunning."

Before long, one of Natalie's paintings, a small piece from the Collard Queen series, was hanging on Belser's wall.

Today, she is working closely with Ron on a new Brookgreen initiative: the Gullah-Geechee Gaarden, a sculpted landscape near the education building that features traditional plants, information panels, oral histories, a bottle tree and artwork curated by Natalie. It will be dedicated on Oct. 13.

The garden is part of Brookgreen's ongoing effort to interpret the African-American experience in Georgetown County, which by 1840 grew nearly half of the total amount of rice produced in all of the United States.

Brookgreen Gardens now is part of the Gullah-Geechee Cultural Heritage Corridor, a federal National Heritage Area established by Congress in 2006 that runs from Wilmington, N.C., to St. Augustine, Fla. One goal of Brookgreen's Gullah programming is to ensure the former rice plantation is an integral part of the corridor, Belser said.

For the Daises, sharing their culture has its rewards, but they bristle at the notion that it's disappearing. Development and gentrification along the sea islands surely presents dangers. After all, a culture is often defined in part by geography, and without a connection to the land that culture can become less cohesive.

But Ron Daise is quick to point out that Gullah *people* are not disappearing.

"It's a still-evolving, living, vibrant culture," he said. "Gullah-Geechee people are here today."

They are the people living on Charleston's East Side, Natalie Daise added. They are the children selling palmetto roses on the Market. They are the people hanging on in the rural outskirts of town.

All the new hotels and restaurants and rising property values make it harder to sustain a sense of community, but that community endures.

"It's a misunderstanding to think it's disappearing," Ron Daise said.

The Chill of Death

Korean War veteran recounts horror of Battle of Chosin

For 50 years John Haffeman kept it bottled up. He felt ashamed, he said.

"I felt a strange feeling, like no one would listen to me if I said anything, so I didn't say a word."

Not to his wife June. Not to his children Diane, Linda Bob and Julie.

He didn't tell them why he had a tendency to experience bursts of impatience and rage. He didn't offer details about the scar on his left elbow. He didn't tell them about the frostbite, the sound of bullets whizzing past his head, the dead man in the sleeping bag, the spilt blood, the day he nearly died.

No, John Haffeman never said much at all about his role in the worst battle of the Korean War, a battle that changed history.

About a dozen years ago, when Haffeman was in his early 70s, he mentioned to a friend that he had seen action in the Battle of Chosin Reservoire when, on Nov. 27, 1950, the Chinese 9th Army surprised U.S. troops gathered in the mountains of the northern Korean peninsula under the command of Maj. Gen. Edward Almond.

The two men attended the same church, and Haffeman's friend encouraged the veteran to share his story with other members. Then about five years ago, Haffeman went to see a Veterans Administration psychiatrist in Augusta who encouraged even more openness.

Haffeman's resolve to unburden himself from the weight of his combat experience was put to the test in November 2015 when The Patriots Point Naval & Maritime Museum commemorated the 65th anniversary of the famous battle. Haffeman was one of three local vets to tell his story. His son Bob, a 58-year-old engineer, was in the audience.

"My son was shocked," Haffeman said.

At 9 p.m. Tuesday, PBS stations will air the two-hour "American

Experience" documentary called "The Battle of Chosin." Haffeman, 85, is one of about 20 veterans interviewed for the program.

These days, it's easy for him to talk about the war, he said. The weight of a 20-ton truck has been lifted. He feels no remorse for what he did, he said, only sadness at the terrible losses and regret at a missed opportunity to thank a fellow Marine for his selflessness.

What happened to Haffeman and his fellow hard chargers in the brutally cold mountains of Korea has become the stuff of legend.

Gung-ho

He was a fresh recruit in the fall of 1950. The U.S. military was so eager to ship their boys to Korea, it made the highly unusual decision to forego boot camp and send new recruits straight to Camp Pendleton in California for 21 days of advanced combat training before putting them on ships crossing the Pacific.

Haffeman was hungry for it, he said. He had grown up in the northeast and recalled collecting tin cans as a kid for the World War II effort. It was then the desire to serve was first manifested. He wanted to be a Marine. He realized in high school he wasn't interested in college so he joined the Marine Corp Reserve.

"It felt good, I was in my element," he said.

He graduated high school in 1950. On June 25, war broke out. He tried to join the service right away but was told to be patient, he would be called up in sequence soon enough. On Sept. 7 he reported for duty. In October he and 2,000 other recruits were shipped to Korea.

"Oh, we were all gung-ho," Haffeman said.

The 1st Marine Division, divided into four regiments, joined thousands of other U.S. X Corps troops on the ground. Under the command of Almond, some of the men trekked northward forming a left plank while others proceeded up the peninsula to the west. They were to convene and secure the north, effectively reuniting a Korea that had been divided in two.

It was cold, and getting colder. Temperatures dropped to 20 degrees below zero, 30 degrees below zero, 40 degrees below zero. The men were well-provisioned, with strong boots and warm sleeping bags, but it was not enough to protect them from the frigid weather. The men opened cans of food only to discover it was frozen solid.

"The only way to unfreeze them was to stick them in a fire," Haffeman said. "We always had a fire going somewhere."

The outside would burn, the inside would remain half-frozen, but the men would wolf the food down anyway.

Delirious

On Nov. 23, Haffeman's division reached the hills near the reservoir and set up encampments. Haffeman, trained as a 16mm mortar man, was handed a heavy Browning Automatic Rifle, which he had never held in his hands before, along with an even heavier vest containing magazines of ammunition. He and the other fighters coped with sporadic gunfire, nuisance fire, from the enemy.

On Nov. 27, he had gathered some tree branches to make a bed when he heard the sound of an ax nearby. Chop! Chop! Chop! Chop! Haffeman pulled on his boots fast. It was getting dark.

And then all hell broke loose.

The air filled with rounds going every which way. Tracer bullets illuminated the smoke-filled air. The battle raged for an hour then stopped. "I thought maybe it's over," Haffeman said. It was not over.

The Chinese, at least 120,000 of them, "came in swarms," wave after wave, attacking a grossly smaller U.N. force of 30,000.

One guy, Haffeman recalled, couldn't get his BAR to fire, so Corporal Fish jumped to his rescue. In the process of unjamming the rifle, Fish shot himself in the foot. The Marines put Fish, bleeding, in a sleeping bag and set him aside while the fighting continued. They could do no more.

"I kept talking to myself: 'You're going to make it, don't worry,'" Haffeman said. Nervously, he lit a cigarette during a brief lull — a bad idea.

Bullets whizzed by constantly. Finally, at 5 a.m. or so, the battlefield quieted. A platoon sergeant kicked Haffeman in the butt. "Shh! We're leaving the hill!" he said. The Marines quietly gathered their gear and grabbed Fish in his sleeping bag, then worked their way down the hill, through the fog of gun powder. Below, the whole valley was full of Chinese corpses.

Officers gathered to strategize. They knew now that the Mao Zedong had deployed Chinese fighters. They knew they were surrounded by the Chinese. They had to decide whether to push the advance to the Yalu River or retreat. Almond wanted to press on. But the dangers were immense and a withdrawal to the 38th parallel seemed the best option. Evacuations of badly wounded troops ensued. Those who could stand on their own fought their way to the retreating convoys.

Haffeman's platoon was assigned to a bitter cold hill where they struggled to clear the enemy and secure the road south. He was instructed to change positions, running along the tree line for cover. BAM! He was hit in the elbow, the bullet severing his artery before splintering the butt of his rifle.

Haffeman was afraid to look. He pulled off his glove and emptied it of blood. Snow was kicking up all around him from Chinese bullets. He rolled away from the machine gun fire, bleeding profusely, and offered his ammo to a fellow Marine.

He found himself next to a lieutenant directing fire at the Chinese roadblock.

"Where'd you get hit?" the lieutenant asked. Haffeman explained. "Well, I can't help you."

Rescued

The wounded 19-year-old was starting to black out when a guy from Item Company came to help. He cut off Haffeman's jacket sleeve and various layers of clothing under it with his bayonet knife and made a tourniquet with a shoelace and stick. He told Haffeman to twist the stick every 10 minutes to loosen the tourniquet and allow a little blood to reach his forearm. "Go to the command post," he instructed.

Haffeman struggled down the hill in a hallucinatory haze. He imagined climbing into a warm sleeping bag and eating canned apricots.

"But something told me no, stay on my feet," he said.

Holding desperately onto tree branches with his good right arm, he stepped across crusty snow, singing, swearing, talking to himself. He was getting delirious. At a frozen stream, his legs began to cramp. The cold alone was killing other men; add to the physical trauma a severe loss of blood and movement became nearly impossible for Haffeman.

Just as he collapsed, the tourniquet slipped off. Corsairs were buzzing over his head like bees. Please God, don't let me die.

He heard the sound of an approaching Jeep, and two men threw him into the back of it. Haffeman said he thinks one of the Corsair pilots saw the trail of blood in the white snow and radioed to base. He was Medics soon staunched the flow of blood and fashioned a cast from chicken wire. Morphine began to ease the pain and the anxiety. Walking wounded, most suffering from frostbite as well as other wounds, were everywhere.

Haffeman slept that night in the back of a warm truck with perhaps six other men. Next morning, he sat in a Jeep with other injured men and joined the convoy south. Every so often, the procession halted to deal with Chinese attacks. At one point, his driver left the vehicle and Chinese fighters descended on the convoy, frozen, frightened, desperate, determined to steal the clothes and supplies from the American dead and wounded.

Haffeman, armed now with a small M1 carbine rifle, rested the barrel on his cast and fired at dozens of Chinese emerging from the trees above the road.

It took a while, but Haffeman made it back to base, received additional treatment for his wound and on Dec. 7 was flown to Japan where surgeons cut out some gangrene and put his elbow back together. His two-month Korean War ordeal was over.

Out of the cold

The Battle of Chosin was both a defeat — U.N. forces failed in their mission to reunite Korea by securing the north — and an odd sort of victory. It forced the retreat of U.N. troops from North Korea, but those troops destroyed or crippled seven large Chinese divisions along the way, and the complex rescue-evacuation operation that followed the three days of heavy fighting at the reservoir is considered among the greatest logistical feats of the U.S. military. The Chinese were resolved to destroy the allied forces but they failed.

After the Battle of Chosin, the war would rage for another two and a half years. In the end, Korea would become the preeminent symbol of a new world order, one that pitted the communist East against the capitalist West during four long decades of the Cold War.

Almond would be vilified by many, even if he was following General Douglas McArthur's orders to forge northward despite the risks. Maj. Gen. Oliver P. Smith, commander of the 1st Marine Division, would be hailed as the level-headed leader who managed to get his men out of a terrible bind.

The 1st Marine Division lost nearly 4,400 men to the fighting and another 7,300 to the cold, including Cpl. Fish in his sleeping bag. The U.S. X Corps and South Korean army lost about 6,000 men.

Haffeman, who spent subsequent decades working as an engineer for AVCO-Lycoming, retired in 1987 at 56 then relocated to the warmth of South Carolina two years later. He has never forgotten the trauma of that frigid winter in late 1950 when he watched his fighting brethren freeze to death, when he narrowly escaped a similar fate. The cold still sits in his bones.

"That's the reason I live here," he said.

From Charleston to New York and Back Again

James Campbell's long reach

James Campbell is 95 years old, and it's time for his favorite local artist to paint his portrait.

So one afternoon Colin Quashie visits Campbell at his James Island home to ask a few questions, to get to know the veteran activist better, to accumulate the ideas that ultimately will fuel his brush strokes.

Quashie paints in a realistic style. He likes to include the wrinkles and signs of arthritis, the manifestations of history on the human form. He captures on canvas his subject's penetrating gaze in such a way that a viewer can recognize interior thought, consciousness, soulforce.

Perhaps that's why Campbell chose Quashie.

The two men have something else in common: a refined injustice detector. They smell racism and tyranny a mile away. They are both animated by the distressing politics of social division. And they have both dedicated themselves to exposing and condemning it.

So Quashie asks his questions from the couch and Campbell, legs crossed, sitting in his favorite chair, coping with the ailments of age, knows he is in good hands.

Consider this: Campbell retired from the New York City school system and returned to Charleston in 1991, at 67 years old. Already he had accumulated more life experiences than most. Already he had helped to integrate the U.S. military, serving as a Montford Point Marine during World War II. Already he had worked in the civil rights movement befriending luminaries such as Jack O'Dell, Bayard Rustin, Malcolm X and Bob Moses. Already he had worked in the theater and contributed to the influential Freedomways journal co-founded by W.E.B. and Shirley Graham Du Bois.

Already he had formed his political worldview, adopting dialectical materialism as the intellectual tool he needed to explain life's social dynamics and injustices. He had lived nine years in Tanzania, teaching and gaining a clearer understanding of post-colonial politics in that part of the world.

After his return home, Campbell kept busy mentoring young people, assisting Moses and Dave Dennis by advancing their Algebra Project initiatives in Lowcountry schools, joining the bioethics committee at the Medical University, working with local labor leaders to improve working conditions.

"You turn the pages of American history and his name is not on any page, but he was present," notes Bobby Donaldson, professor of African American history at the University of South Carolina. "Talk about Malcolm X, Jim knew him well. Fannie Lou Hamer, Langston Hughes. How many people have letters from Langston Hughes in their collection?"

Indeed, James Campbell walks the walk.

On the path

It took him a while to find his stride. Growing up in Charleston, in a cottage on President Street that eventually was demolished to make way for the Crosstown expressway, he was a normal kid, playing in the yard, exploring the neighborhood, going to school. His father, James Campbell Sr., was a farmer and railroad fireman from Hopkins, S.C., who moved to Charleston and became an ambulance driver for Roper Hospital, which catered to white patients. He also served as a driver for funerals. His mother, Eva Juliette Jones Campbell, graduated from the Avery Normal Institute in 1916, along with Septima Poinsette Clark, served as a teacher for a while, then devoted herself to family.

Campbell remembers playing in front of the house while his grandmother Millie Cole sat on the porch smoking a corncob pipe and seeing the distant past as clear as day. "The buckras!" she would exclaim in a voice of angry condemnation. What she saw in her mind's eye was her own mother, Eliza Davis, whipped by the slave master in the years before the Civil War, a scene she witnessed when she was perhaps 14 or 15 years old.

"It made me stop my play and just look," he said.

Millie Cole would take her grandson to church, a frightening experience that often lasted all day.

"I came to realize that people in that congregation were her age and older," he said. Most had been enslaved in their youth, freed in 1865, possessing nothing but a sense of solidarity and a will to persist.

The Campbells were members of the NAACP. They contributed to an African aid fund. They kept themselves informed and ensured their five children (Jim was the oldest) visited the Dart Library. Jim would sneak away sometimes to swim or fish, but the smell of pluff mud would give him away.

"You stinkin' to high heaven!" his mother would say admonishingly.

Young Campbell's mother and his Aunt Sadie pushed him to learn, and eventually pushed him out of the dirt streets of Gadsden Green and onto a sturdier, if winding, path that led him far away from Charleston.

"They put ideas in my head about going away to school," he said. They knew that a good high school education would lead to college, and that college would lead to a better life.

He thought he might become a boarder at the Tuskegee Institute, but there was no place for him there.

"Eva, that boy can go to Voorhees in Denmark," his Aunt Sadie declared one day.

Denmark! That is really far away, Campbell thought to himself. "Oh my goodness, I'm out of here!"

Then he learned that, no, Denmark was a small rural town about 100 miles away, near Orangeburg, and he was a little disappointed.

But Voorhees Normal and Industrial Institute, and its students who hailed from Detroit and Philadelphia and Washington, D.C., and Columbia, opened his eyes. And his English teacher, Mrs. Catherine Booker, encouraged him to discuss ideas, interpret texts, think critically. She opened young Campbell's mind.

Teaching and learning

In 1942, his senior year at Voorhees, he was drafted. He wanted to join the Air Force, but when he learned it was segregated he joined the 52nd Marine Defense Battalion instead and prepared for war in the Pacific theater. He trained, took courses, awakened to the violence of the world, drew connections between Nazi and Japanese tyranny and the African-American experience.

He was about to ship out for the planned Japanese invasion when the U.S. dropped its two atom bombs, ending the war in the Pacific.

After he was discharged, he passed his GED and enrolled at Morgan State University in Baltimore, interrupted when he was called back to active duty during the Korean Police Action. Again he saw no action. Rather, he took courses, read books and became "anti-war," he said.

At Morgan he majored in English and minored on theater, finding his way to the stage of the Arena Players and, eventually, securing an audition at the famed Actor's Studio in New York City. He didn't get in, but the idea of acting on Broadway took hold. After a couple years of teaching in Baltimore, he left for the bright lights of the Big Apple in 1957, studied acting with Uta Hagen, met leftists who had been black-listed by Sen. Joseph McCarthy, and found a part-time job serving summons for a small company run by a politically progressive Jewish man with whom Campbell engaged in conversations about American racism.

He filled his brain, molded his thoughts, formed his opinions.

Then things started happening fast. He got his first substitute teaching job at a junior high school in the South Bronx, learned about the United Federation of Teachers and got involved, met all sorts of people.

"You're either White or Black in the South," he said. "But up north, there are Italians, Hungarians, Irish, Jews…"

He exceled in his teaching career, securing permanent positions and working hard in the classroom during the day. In the evenings he dashed downtown to attend acting classes. He would return home around 10:30 p.m., prepare for school the next day, then sleep. After a while, Campbell formed his own acting troupe, which performed one-act plays by Tennessee Williams, Thorton Wilder and others in the sanctuaries of churches and the gymnasiums of YMCAs. The troupe, along with Campbell's devotion to acting, eventually evaporated.

But by then he was immersed in the civil rights movement.

Awestruck

In 1958, he came across a newspaper headline he liked — "Heed their rising voices" — and thought it would make a good button. After identifying a button-maker in Lower Manhattan, Campbell visited Bayard Rustin of the Southern Christian Leadership Conference at his Harlem office with his offering. Rustin liked the idea but not the slogan and ended up changing the text, Campbell said.

Jack O'Dell was there and invited Campbell to help out in the office. O'Dell, a SCLC advisor and strategist and known leftist, was looking for a new place to live. Campbell had just moved into a big rent-controlled apartment, a fifth-floor walkup at 135th Street and St. Nicholas Avenue, and was happy to rent a room to his new friend. It was largely through O'Dell that Campbell gained full access to the freedom movement and exercised his political intellect.

By the late 1950s, his embrace of Marxist philosophy, especially dialectical materialism, was tightening. This philosophy expounded that we live in a material reality whose contradictions are generated and explained by real-world conditions: class, work, economic interaction. Even the human mind is subject to these conditions. Our thoughts are not independent or metaphysical; they are shaped by our socio-economic circumstances.

This is why Campbell rejoices when he reads the Latin phrase posted above the door of the Medical University's morgue and autopsy room: "This place is where Death rejoices to come to the aid of Life." What could be more dialectically material? It's why he decided to donate his body for medical research, he said.

O'Dell was associated with the Communist Party which threatened to taint SCLC and compromise Martin Luther King Jr.'s influence. By 1963, the year of the March on Washington, he had been pushed to the margins, along with other avowed leftists in the movement. Years later, in the 1980s, O'Dell would become a campaign advisor to presidential candidate Jesse Jackson.

Campbell, meanwhile, was becoming fascinated with Malcolm X, who by 1963 was in an increasingly strained relationship with the Nation of Islam.

"I was starting to pay attention," Campbell recalled. "I was impressed with his ability to speak to the working class." Malcolm echoed Aesop when he employed animals in his rhetoric to illustrate a point. "People in the street need a reference they can understand," Campbell said. After a 1964 rally in Harlem, he introduced himself. "I was impressed by how quiet and polite he was."

Soon, Campbell, ever the multitasker (he was pursuing his master's degree at the City University of New York and Bank Street College during this period), was designing the program for what he and Malcolm called a Liberation School, and teaching small groups of students about the African liberation movement, capitalism's impacts and the power of enlightened thought.

One day, not long after Malcolm's house had been firebombed, Campbell invited him to breakfast at the Harlem apartment where Malcolm could meet Jack O'Dell. They chatted casually about this and that. Campbell asked Malcolm about his family.

"Brother, let me give you Betty's telephone number, because you are someone I want her to stay in touch with," Malcolm said to Campbell, sensing his days were numbered. About one week later, he was murdered at the Audubon Ballroom.

But it was Paul Robeson who left the greatest impression on Campbell. The singer-activist had emerged from retirement to give a concert in a New York City hotel, and Campbell's assignment from Freedomways was to interview him and write the program notes. Here was a towering intellect of the Left and a great artist, the man who inspired Campbell to try his hand at acting, the man who articulated so well the plight of African Americans and who placed that plight in a global context.

"I was so awestruck because I had been reading about him, and W.E.B. Du Bois, all my life," Campbell said. "I couldn't get over the fact that I was in his presence."

James Baldwin was to make the introduction at the event, and Campbell was assigned to make sure Baldwin arrived on time and made it to the stage.

In Africa

Campbell had been studying the writings of Julius Nyerere, the Tanzanian anti-colonial activist and politician, and decided in 1973 to go abroad. Campbell was intrigued by how Nyerere and other African rev-

olutionaries were applying leftist politics to the construction of post-colonial states, and how two forces — African nationalism and Pan-Afri-
canism — interacted. Campbell favored the latter. He had spent some
time in the late 1960s working with Student Nonviolent Coordinating
Committee activists to develop a curriculum to help Black people interested in moving to Africa.

Now he was one of those people.

"I saw it as an opportunity to invest in a new country, (to build)
something strong and new and alternative to the problems we face
here," he said.

He spent nine years there, teaching English first in Bihawana and then
at the International School in Dar es Salaam. The experience had its pros
and cons. He was never allowed to forget that he was an American visi-
tor, no matter his contributions, he said. Eventually, he concluded that he
should be fighting for freedom and democracy at home in the U.S.

First he came to Charleston, in time to say farewell to his dying
mother. He taught briefly at Burke High School then returned to New
York, where he became assistant principal at two Harlem middle schools
and then district coordinator for social studies until his retirement in
1991. He came home to Charleston and began a new, long chapter of
his life.

In Charleston, Campbell got involved in labor issues, working with
members of the International Longshoreman's Association, he joined
the Medical University's bioethics team as a member-at-large, and he
became involved with Bob Moses' Algebra Project.

He also served on the advisory board of the College of Charleston's
School of Education, and was chairman of the education committee for
the Charleston branch of the NAACP. He kept busy.

Keeping busy

Dave Dennis first met Campbell in Mississippi during the summer of
1964, when many activists joined the effort to get Black people reg-
istered to vote. But it wasn't until the early 1990s that the two men
became colleagues and friends.

Dennis was southern coordinator for the Algebra Project, a math literacy organization that works with low-income youth. He and Campbell

set up programs on St. Helena Island, in Savannah, in the Charleston area and in Weldon, N.C.

"We called him *Mzee*," Dennis said, invoking the Swahili honorific, "the elder of the movement, the person civil rights veterans go to for advice. ... Students liked him because he told stories. At the same time, he understood community organizing, so he could get families involved."

When they visited project sites, local people would host a buffet lunch.

"People began to compete around the food," Dennis recalled. "The center of attraction among middle-aged ladies was Jim. Everyone else was with paper plates, and here's Jim with china and silverware."

When Campbell attended staff retreats, he generally held forth like Socrates.

"Jim just started telling stories, until lunch," Dennis said. "He had talked for two and half hours. We just sat there listening to him."

Mary Faith Marshall, director of the Center for Health Humanities and Ethics and director of the Program in Biomedical Ethics at the University of Virginia School of Medicine, remembers Campbell from her days leading the nascent bioethics program at MUSC.

She and her colleagues wanted someone on the committee who could provide an outsider's perspective.

"Jim was just the perfect person," she said. "He was such a delightful man, but he also brought the community to the table, which is really important. Ethics consultants are mostly clinicians who work in hospital and are acculturated to that life, we see things through lens that's too narrow. Jim helped us ensure we had a broader view of the issues at hand and the people involved."

This was especially important given the scandal underway at MUSC at the time. The institution was being sued for its policy of testing pregnant African American women for drug use. The lawsuit, Ferguson v. Charleston, eventually was appealed to the Supreme Court, which decided in favor of the women.

Marshall, armed with advice she received from Campbell, was subpoenaed and condemned the racially motivated practice in her testimony — which cost her her job.

"(Jim) was the soul of the consult service and the ethics committee," she said. "He gave folks a lot of courage, and a spine that they needed."

It was Campbell who nominated Marshall for the Charleston NAACP's Pathfinder Award.

"That is the most important honor I have ever gotten in my life, and that's because of Jim Campbell," she said.

Daron Lee Calhoun II, an administrator at the Avery Research Center who coordinates programming and the Race and Social Justice Initiative, called Campbell a mentor and role model who demonstrates the importance of research-based activism.

"Jim Campbell is the guy who made me the activist I am today," Calhoun said. Understanding political movements is the only reliable way to make the necessary connections between history and lived experience, he added. "He is one of the most prophetic people, and one of the most intellectually based people, I have every met in my life."

So when the Avery received an anonymous donation in 2019, it used the money to bolster the Racial and Social Justice Initiative grant program, which provides students with financial awards and opportunities to learn teaching literacy, grant writing, social justice work, interviewing techniques and more, Calhoun said.

It was immediately obvious to him that the award should be named in honor of his mentor. The student recipients would be called "Campbell Scholars."

"Not only has he lived so long, it's been a journey, a Great Migration story," Bobby Donaldson of the University of South Carolina said. "Charleston to Denmark to Baltimore to New York to Africa. Through his own journey one could trace the diaspora."

Now, at home, he sits in his wicker chair in the corner of his living room. Books and magazines are piled on the coffee table. Colin Quashie is there asking questions and taking pictures he can reference later as he sketches and paints. The master teacher, 95 years old, smiles and speaks of his life.

The Odyssey

From Liberia to the Lowcountry, mayhem to music-making

Ten years ago, when the two boys were 10 and 8 respectively, they left one world and entered another. Before, there was dismay, fear, mischief and terror, along with strong bonds of friendship. After, there was green grass, music lessons, electric power, Legos and safety.

And family. Finally, there was family.

Here's an episode that's among Ezekiel's earliest memories: He was 3 years old. His father and brother said, "We're going somewhere," and the next thing he knew he was at an orphanage. "This is where you are going to be living now," his father told him.

At the Buchanan Mission, Ezekiel cried for a week, uncertain of everything. He spoke only the native language of Grand Bassa county in Liberia. "I didn't know an ounce of English," he said. "These were all strange people, a strange place, strange food." He was in the middle of nowhere, a remote, dusty region of a brutalized West African country. He was there for more than two years.

Eventually, another boy arrived at the mission, two years younger and lost. John's mother had dropped him off on the road that ran by the building. It was a well-used thruway on which trucks passed regularly. John stood there, dumbstruck, confused by his abandonment, then sadly meandered in the roadway as a truck rumbled toward him.

A few other boys were nearby. One was watching John, aware of the danger, and he sprang into action. It wasn't long after Ezekiel pulled the newcomer from the street that another boy was struck by a passing car. This was a perilous place, soon to become much more dangerous.

The two boys immediately became fast friends, Zeke the older protector and a charismatic leader in the orphanage, John the quiet ward. They found a way to get through each day in this remote outpost. Until the brutal second civil war burst in.

Nurturing talent

Lately, Ezekiel has been working on the beautiful violin entr'acte "Meditation" from Massenet's opera "Thais." It has a gorgeous soaring melody and requires both technical control and emotional sweep. John has been playing Franz Liszt's Sonetto 104 del Petrarca, a bold work that references a poem by the great Italian writer Petrarch.

The young men are talented, and serious about their music. Zeke, now 20, is studying with Lee-Chin Siow at the College of Charleston. John, 18, is studying with Irina Pevzner at the Charleston Academy of Music.

They dabbled in music back in Liberia, Zeke especially, who was a pretty good drummer. But it wasn't until about eight years ago that they took their first deliberate steps into the domain of classical music.

It started at home, in Moncks Corner. Janet and Gene DiMaria were homeschooing their three biological sons, Geno, Dominic and Anthony, and learning a musical instrument was part of the process. They started on piano, an instrument that stuck with Geno; Dominic migrated to guitar and Anthony to violin.

The older boys helped teach Zeke and John piano. Zeke kind of hated it and embraced violin instead. John took to the keys like a penguin to icy water.

Soon, Zeke moved on to the Suzuki books for violin, then knuckled down a few years later when a family friend and violinist began to teach him privately. In 2011, Zeke went off to string camp, then settled into the private studio of DeAnndra Drewry-Glenn, with whom he studied for four years until enrolling at the College of Charleston.

John got his start at the piano with his brother Geno, then signed up for private lessons with Scott McDowell, who taught the up-and-comer some theory and jazz improvisation. John listened to a lot of music — soundtracks, hymns — and made his own arrangements.

He was getting good, playing some wedding and restaurant gigs, and listening to the music of J.S. Bach. By 2014, he was entering competitions and practicing on nice pianos at Fox Music. Owner Charles Fox suggested he contact Pevzner, one of the area's best teachers.

Command to shoot

The boys were not really aware of the war, though a Guinea-backed rebel group had been stirring things up in the north of the country since 1999. This was a new round of fighting. The first civil war, which began in 1989, was a bloody, fractious, eight-year-long power shift that overthrew what many considered the illegitimate government of Samuel Doe, who had led a coup d'etat nine years earlier. By 1997, a peace accord was achieved, Doe was executed and Charles Taylor was elected president. About 600,000 people had died as a result of the fighting.

The second civil war fired up just two years later, with rebel forces challenging Taylor and his government. Zeke and John remember the day a rebel general arrived at the orphanage with his troops.

"They lined up the orphans against the wall, pointing guns at us," Zeke said. It was likely supposed to be a massacre. The firing squad was in position. About 500 terrified children stood along a wall just outside the building. "The general was supposed to give the command to shoot but couldn't," Zeke recalled. "He broke down crying."

Instead, he issued a threat: Get these children out of here now or we will kill them all.

They traipsed through the dust to Daniel Hoover Children's Village, where they stayed briefly, then on to a U.N. safe house near the capital of Monrovia. They did not eat for days. "I was so hungry I could not even walk," Zeke said. "I had to crawl down the stairs, I felt really dizzy. I got a handful of rice from one of the matrons and that was enough to bring me back."

They listened to the tanks rumbling by, shooting in the streets (some from child soldiers recruited by both sides), and U.N. helicopters passing overhead. After a while, they returned to the Children's Village, where they remained for about two more years.

A natural flair

Pevzner is an accomplished performer and selective teacher, active with Chamber Music Charleston and in charge of the Charleston Academy of Music. She said she is impressed by John's dedication.

"He wakes up at 6 a.m. and goes to practice," she said. He will continue for hours if uninterrupted. His mother, Janet DiMaria, must stop him so he can turn some attention to academics and other subjects. "I've never seen anything like it."

But dedication alone does not make an artist.

"When I see him play — I can't put it into words — the expression comes from a different world," Pevzner said. "It's something I didn't teach him. He's one of those people who can be more than a musician. He can tell another kind of story with his music. ... I really think John has that power."

And besides playing the piano, John makes bold and fascinating paintings, accumulating a portfolio that might come in handy one day.

Lee-Chin, a violin professor at the College of Charleston, said she first got to know about Zeke from Drewry-Glenn, a former student.

"When I first heard Ezekiel, I saw great potential in him," she said. "His passion for music was palpable. He has a natural flair as a performer, and stands out with his unique musical voice. I was very moved that his parents had given him and his brother the gift of a family and a fine education."

Lee-Chin wanted to nurture the young man's talents and recruited him to join the music program at the college.

"He fits in perfectly in my studio, which has a great mix of international and local students," she said. "He has an outgoing personality and we have a great rapport. He is a joy to teach. Besides playing the violin, he is also a talented cook."

Double adoption

Gene and Janet DiMaria spent years in Arizona before they moved to the Lowcountry in 2005 when Gene DiMaria landed a new job as firearms and safety officer with the Probation and Pre-Trial Services Office of the U.S. Courts, located on the old Navy base.

The couple had three sons and experience as foster parents. They had long wanted to adopt, Janet DiMaria said. By 2005, when they got serious about adoption, Liberia had become a focal point, partly because of the terrible toll of two civil wars and the many orphans that resulted.

It was no easy task. The bureaucracy was thick. Liberian authorities threw up obstacles, fearful of those who sought to exploit the situation.

Human trafficking was a genuine concern. The adoption process was supposed to take six to nine months. It took two years.

With support from their three boys, the couple had plans to adopt a single child in Liberia. Geno chimed in: Maybe bringing back just one boy would make it tough for him to adjust. The family thought about it. Then, that same night, they received an email from the adoption agency informing them that the boy they were to pick up, Ezekiel, had a best friend. They were practically attached at the hip.

Suddenly, plans changed.

At Daniel Hoover Children's Village, the orphans were increasingly aware of the white visitors (they were always white) who occasionally stopped by to take one of the boys away. "We had heard about adoptions before," John said. But they were naturally skeptical. Sometimes they would get word that an adoption was imminent then experience a delay or change. The authorities would announce adoptions only on the day children were scheduled to be picked up.

One day, Zeke, and a few others went to the market. On the way back the group ran into a kid from the mission who told him, "White people are here, you're going to be adopted." Zeke didn't believe the boy. But it was true. John was eating lunch (he never missed a meal); Zeke returned too late to finish his food or to say a proper farewell to all his friends. He and John were whisked away.

"I remember being really, really sad; I was leaving all my friends," he said. "When I got in the car, sadness started building up and building up."

It was not a joyful moment but instead another profound and un-settling change, another trauma. What was happening? Where were they going?

Across continents

The situation was very complicated. The DiMarias relied on a friend, Paige, who also was adopting two children in Liberia. Paige gathered all the young adoptees and left Liberia on a Tuesday night, but not without running into trouble. She paid extortion money to Nigerian rebels in Senegal who delayed the group's arrival at the international airport. They finally flew to Belgium, where the boys saw their first snowfall, then to Chicago, arriving Friday morning. The DiMarias assisted with logistics and helped pay for the flights.

Ezekiel snagged a seat in first class where he was served some strange cold, creamy, sweet substance that he didn't like and where he watched the movie "Blood Diamond."

In Chicago, they were transferred from Paige to the DiMarias. Another trauma. In a short time, the boys had grown close to their reassuring escort, and the airport transition, the latest in a string of tumultuous developments, provoked tears.

In Moncks Corner, the mysteries of a foreign land slowly dissolved. "We had heard stories about coming to America," John said. "That they put you in a freezer and you turn white. We thought that Spider-Man was real, that 'The Matrix' was real. We heard that all is free in America."

No, all is not free in America, Gene and Janet told the two boys. One must earn a living, pay for everything. But then they'd go to the doctor and get free candy (then sell it back to members of the family). They'd get gifts from friends and neighbors. Eventually they caught on though, said Gene DiMaria.

When they arrived in the Lowcountry, they were ill and underweight, depressed, anxious. Zeke weighed 48 pounds, John 46. They struggled with malaria and ringworm. The family went through hundreds of washcloths and paper towels. Nothing could be reused. Clothing and bedding had to be washed constantly. They were tired all the time. It took a couple of months for them to gain their footing.

Their presence also was unsettling at first to their older brothers. Reality has a way of rolling roughshod over the imagination. This was not exactly like what they had expected. "These guys required so much care and focus, I felt like I was treading water," Dominic recalled.

John and Zeke were afraid of the dachshund, which had a tendency to nip at people. John, who didn't speak clearly, would succumb to tantrums that initially required Zeke to act as interpreter. "He's mad," Zeke would explain.

They had to learn all the basic things — about privacy and ownership and responsibility, about the cost of things such as electricity, about vacuum cleaners, about closing the bathroom door and flushing the toilet paper.

And then there were the terrifying nightmares that troubled both boys and tended to come in waves. They only subsided after some intensive praying among family and friends, though both continue to experience bad dreams occasionally.

Getting up to speed

The DiMarias were not entirely surprised by all this. "We did the research ahead of time," Gene DiMaria said. "We knew things would get broken."

The boys would spend hours constructing complex Lego structures, replete with small lights they powered with built-in batteries. They created a playhouse from cardboard, sticks and twine, meticulously sewing it all together.

"They were the most patient young men I've ever seen," Gene DiMaria said.

Little by little, they gained their health, put on weight, got to know their new extended family, grew accustomed to the way things worked in the U.S. and began to pursue their artistic interests. They were quickly embraced by their older brothers, all of whom became filmmakers.

Today, John is thinking about college, painting pictures and playing pieces on the piano that challenge both his technique and his emotional investment. Ezekiel is at the College of Charleston, studying hard and practicing violin. Sometimes they perform together.

Zeke is adjusting to college. To prepare for it, he enrolled in SPECTRA (Speedy Consolidation and Transition Program), a summer curriculum mostly populated by African Americans. When classmates found out Zeke was adopted by a white couple, they accused him of not being truly black, and Zeke, a native African, felt he had to defend himself. The skepticism among his peers soon faded.

This weekend, the family celebrated the 10th anniversary of the boys' arrival. It's been an adventure, with more adventure to come.

The ringworm is long gone. The nightmares are infrequent. The vacuum cleaner is a familiar object now.

Zeke is making the violin sing. John is bringing the piano to life. Their future is filled with promise.

Nelson B. Rivers III

From protester to pastor

"What time is it?" the preacher asks.

"Preaching time!" comes the collective response.

"What time is it?" he repeats.

"Preaching time!!" they answer, louder.

"What time is it?"

"Preaching time!!!"

"Gospel means 'good news,' and there's no better news than the Book of John," the Rev. Nelson B. Rivers III begins, steering the congregation at Charity Missionary Baptist Church to Chapter 9, Verses 18-25, which recount the story of the blind man made to see.

The preacher is electric. The people shout out, stand up. Rivers, an ordained pastor for 10 years, a political activist for 40, most of which was spent rising through the ranks of the NAACP, has found a new path to trod, a new calling to obey, a new arena to fill with his spirited cry, a new reason to speak out and speak loudly.

The new reason is not unlike the old reason. He has always strived to decry injustice and light the path toward liberation. The difference now is that Charity is his new home, and faith furnishes his vocabulary.

Formation

"In a time of peace, you need an army to keep the peace; in a time of war, you need an army to fight your battles," Rivers said by way of explaining why the National Association for the Advancement of Colored People keeps on keeping on.

Currently, he serves as the organization's vice president of stakeholder relations. The NAACP is celebrating its centennial this year.

Rivers, 58, born in Bennett's Point in Colleton County, raised there and in Charleston, came of age during the tumultuous 1960s. When he was 12, his family attended St. Paul Baptist Church on Rutledge Avenue and heard the mighty preaching of the Rev. James A. Williams. Years later, it was that unforgettable voice Rivers would emulate.

He was 17 when he read "The Autobiography of Malcolm X." An obsessive reader during those years, this was the first book he encountered that described with such raw honesty the life of a black man, and it radicalized him, he said.

These were the days he played the trumpet and baritone horn in the Burke High School Band. These were the days he combated arrogance and privilege, embracing the idea of civil disobedience, direct action and loud protest.

It was 1968. That April, Martin Luther King Jr. was assassinated. That June, Robert F. Kennedy was killed. It was chaotic in America when Rivers left Charleston for Wilberforce University in Ohio, a school co-founded by Daniel Alexander Payne in 1856.

Payne, who became the first black president of the first black college founded by blacks, was born in Charleston, where he started a school at age 18, a school he was forced to close when, in 1835, South Carolina passed a law making it illegal to teach blacks to read.

By the time Rivers arrived at Wilberforce, his mind was saturated with biographies, histories and science fiction novels, especially the work of Isaac Asimov. He knew all about Thomas Jefferson, Ben Franklin, George Washington, the American Indian Wars, interstellar empires, robots and Martians.

And, committed to the cause of empowering the oppressed, he became an organizer and protester.

"I became the blackest thing on campus," he said. "Black was everything."

He called for a boycott of the university, complaining that black history was insufficiently taught, that the three-strike penalty system and evening curfews were unfair, that the trustee board ought to include a student representative.

He disparaged the NAACP for being "too moderate, too Uncle Tom." He praised the Black Panther Party. He considered membership in the Nation of Islam. He faulted friends and colleagues if they hesitated to join black organizations on campus.

"You're not black if you don't join," he told one friend, enraged.

Then, a week or two later, someone tried to persuade Rivers to join the Black Liberation Front. When Rivers hesitated, the man said, "You're not black if you don't join." Rivers heard the echo of his own voice, and he began to question his motivation, allegiances and attitudes.

Then he participated in a class debate, defending the views of Booker T. Washington against the ideas of W.E.B. DuBois (which he favored). The debate was enlightening, he said. Although he remained unconvinced by Washington's arguments and actions, he understood that they were made without malice and helped advance the cause of oppressed black people.

Something else happened during this period that challenged Rivers' orthodoxy. His Black Panther friends were getting thrown in jail and couldn't raise enough money to cover the bond set by the court. Only one organization succeeded in freeing them and defending their rights: the NAACP.

The cigarette salesman

A man must earn a living, so Rivers went to work for Liberty Mutual, settling insurance claims up to $10,000 in the nearly all-white town of Rocky River outside Cleveland. He hated the cold; he hated the job. So in September 1974, he returned to Charleston and applied for a job with the Great American Life Insurance Co. When he told the hiring manager he was capable of settling claims of up to $10,000, the man refused to believe it.

"I had to recalibrate my thinking," Rivers said.

He found work with Brown & Williamson, maker of Kool, Lucky Strike, Pall Mall and many other cigarette brands. Rivers said he was the company's first black sales rep. He was with B&W for nine years until 1984. (Five years later, the company would hire Jeffrey Wigand as its vice president of research and development. Wigand would become a whistleblower made famous by a "60 Minutes" investigation that contributed to the massive Medicaid suit and $368 billion settlement against the tobacco companies.)

As a cigarette salesman, Rivers traveled extensively throughout the state, getting to know its urban centers, back roads and small towns. It was good preparation for his future work as an NAACP organizer.

During those salesman days, Rivers and a few others decided they wanted to establish a new NAACP branch downtown to revitalize the mission of the civil rights organization in Charleston. But there was already a functioning branch, and they couldn't have two.

In North Charleston, though, the branch was inactive, so Rivers and his colleagues got busy. A young man was vying for president against the Rev. Willie Davenport, the experienced pastor at Royal Baptist Church. Though Rivers and his colleagues backed the younger man, hoping that fresh blood would reinvigorate the branch, Davenport had a roomful of supporters and won handily, Rivers said.

Rivers credited the loss to a lack of familiarity with the nominating rules. "He was not cheating me, but he was beating me because he knew the rules," Rivers said of the victorious pastor whom, later, he would befriend. "I vowed never to lose again because of the rules."

In 1978, Davenport appointed Rivers as first vice president and youth adviser. In 1980, Davenport decided to step down and throw his support behind Rivers, who became branch director. A poised, capable leader who knew how to energize the community, Rivers was positioned to rise rapidly through the ranks of the organization.

In 1984, he was elected director of the state conference, succeeding Ike Williams. The issues he had to contend with were many: a Confederate battle flag mounted atop the S.C. Statehouse, education disparities, diluted representation in the state Legislature, lack of business opportunities for blacks, chronic discrimination, ongoing incidents of illegal segregation and more.

"It was a critical time for the state conference," said James Gallman, who was Aiken branch president 1988-97 and state president 1998-2004.

Gallman said he remembers Rivers as always being ready to take the lead anywhere in the state.

The two men, along with four others, visited the Buffalo Room restaurant in North Augusta in 1989 after hearing that the restaurant refused to serve blacks.

"We decided to go to check this out," Gallman said.

When they arrived, the owner came running out, cursing and

threatening to strike the men with a big pot. A trial judge, warning that such behavior should have been expected, nevertheless awarded the plaintiffs $100,000, which was never paid, Gallman said.

On another occasion, Rivers joined Gallman in Aiken after a group of young black men were told they could not swim in a private, "whites-only" area of Richardsons Lake. The owners called the NAACP the next morning to apologize for their employee's actions, and a face-to-face meeting quickly was set up for that afternoon. Rivers brought one of his young daughters, who splashed in the water nearby as the men talked.

Rivers was vigilant, talented, well-versed in the issues and a capable speaker and organizer, Gallman said. "With most direct action, Nelson would be our point man," he said.

Rivers said one of his proudest accomplishments was the NAACP's role in the transformation of at-large voting systems to single-member districts that helped correct decades of black under-representation in several governments. Between 1986 and 1994, the number of elected black officials increased by about 300, he said.

By 1988, state membership in the NAACP increased from 8,000 to 37,000, then leveled out at about 22,000, Rivers said.

No fools here

The Rev. Joseph A. Darby, pastor of Morris Brown AME Church and who has been long active in the NAACP, knew Rivers when both men lived in Columbia. Darby said his charismatic colleague is expert at formulating solid arguments that are difficult to dispute.

"He's an impressive brother, very articulate, very poised," Darby said. "He's not one with much tolerance for — what's the word? — he doesn't suffer fools wisely."

In 1994, Rivers was promoted to Southeast regional director. In 1999, he became national chief of field operations. In 2002, he assumed the mantle of chief operating officer. In 2006 and 2008, he was a serious candidate for president of the organization.

Then, last year, Rivers decided it was time to come home. He had been serving as associate pastor of St. Paul Baptist Church for nearly five years, working under the Rev. William Tindal. The desire to pastor full time had been brewing for a while, he said, and he was willing to continue as associate, or find another position somewhere else. A church in California offered him a job, but the West Coast was not God's plan, he said.

He heard about Charity Missionary Baptist Church, rooted in the Liberty Hill neighborhood he knew so well from his days as the North Charleston NAACP leader, a church that was home to friends and colleagues, a sanctuary in which the strong words of the Rev. B.J. Whipper once rang out. Rivers announced to Charity's leadership that he wanted to be their pastor.

Looking forward

Along the journey, Rivers has made some enemies; those who resent his stinging recriminations, his dogged persistence in fighting against what he perceives to be unjust, his ever-incisive firebrand rhetoric. And, of course, he has made many friends.

The Rev. Al Sharpton came to Charleston last month at Rivers' invitation to preach at Charity Baptist's "Celebration of Unity" gala and banquet. Today, the Rev. Jesse Jackson will visit the Lowcountry to preach in honor of his friend's one-year anniversary as pastor of Charity.

Such connections make Rivers an asset and a potential risk: Some in the congregation have worried that their new pastor will bring politics to the pulpit, according to Rossilind Daniels, Charity's minister of music and a member since childhood.

Expectations are high. Charity was without a pastor for more than a year before Rivers joined, and without steady leadership since the Rev. Jay Charles Levy left in 2005 after nine years at the helm, Daniels said. Attendance had been in decline. About half of the church's 300 members left when Levy ended his tenure, she said.

Today, membership is on the rise, and worries are appeased.

Rivers has focused on building the body of Christ, not a political movement, Daniels said. There have been no calls for boycotts from the pulpit, only a spirit-filled preacher imploring the congregation to listen to the word of God, she said.

"The Lord has told him, 'Here's your new venue, this is your new walk, to be pastor,'" she said.

Darby said his friend's charisma, intelligence and organizing skills can be applied effectively within the church.

"Hopefully, he will be one of those people who can bring about some of the needed cooperation among clergy in Charleston," Darby said.

At 58, Rivers has much left to do. He has a new flock, a vision to strengthen Charity, a determination to bring people together to share the good news and improve their lives. He will preach inspired by the memory of his mentors and role models: the Rev. James A. Williams, his childhood pastor; the Rev. Julius C. Hope, who was president of the Georgia State Conference of the NAACP and director of religious affairs for the national NAACP; the Rev. Dr. Howard W. Creecy, who a decade ago ordained Rivers at Olivet Baptist Church of Christ in Fayetteville, Ga.

His family is with him: wife Carolyn; son Sonni Ali; daughters Dana, Tamara Carin and Jamilia Ayana; and his four grandchildren.

'Now I see'

In the sanctuary on a recent Sunday, the congregation is rapt with attention, responding to Rivers' sermon with bursts of vocal affirmations.

It's a common idea that God punishes us for our sins by making us suffer, he tells them. But this isn't true.

"The Lord doesn't pay you back like that," he says. "Some think the Lord is your hitman, you can sic him on somebody."

Laughter.

But maybe we suffer so that when suffering ceases we know whom to credit. "It might be when you get in trouble, and you get out of trouble, God can get the glory!"

The Pharisees wanted to know how Jesus cured the blind man, he says.

"But it doesn't matter how he did it; what matters is that he did it!"

And what did the blind man answer, when threatened with expulsion from the synagogue should he confess the "sin" of acknowledging Christ's miracle?

"Whether he is a sinner or not, I know not. One thing I know. Whereas I was blind, now I see."

We cannot see God, but we must trust him, Rivers says, raising his voice louder and louder.

"Whereas I was blind, now I see!" Rivers says. "Now — I — see!"

Pat Conroy Talks

Beloved S.C. author, turning 70, forced to endure celebration and praise

In a sprawling conversation over a healthy lunch at the Beaufort Inn, beloved South Carolina raconteur Pat Conroy's musings became exquisitely purposeful when he was asked to contemplate food.

You must bear in mind that, two years ago, the Dark Angel was hovering about our writer of tall tales in uncomfortable proximity. Conroy's renowned hedonism had caught up with him: he was very ill and generating concerned buzz in literary circles across the state.

Since then, he's found a personal trainer, Mina Truong, who thrills in reminding her client of death in more ways than one, five days a week. Sometimes during his exercise sessions, he wonders if he made the wrong devil's bargain. But the doubts soon dissipate, for Pat Conroy is doing much better. Nowadays, he sticks to salads and unsweetened ice tea, reserving certain of life's riches for his imagination and his stories.

So when asked about his ideal meal, he glanced at his salad ménage-a-trois and set down his fork, relishing the opportunity to think deeply about the matter, envisioning the answer in his mind's eye. Slowly, carefully, he described five courses:

"Let me start off with Beluga caviar," he said. "I want it on a cracker like a communion wafer, with unpasteurized sour cream from Russia, white onion chopped fine, the Beluga stacked in its glistening eggs and scented with lemon."

That was the starter. For the second course he recalled Italy, where he lived for two years in the early 1980s. "I would like the beef tartar from Trattoria al Pantheon in Rome."

Then it was on to the Deep South. "And let me have for the next course, the fish course, the lobster made in Frank Stitt's restaurant, the Highlands Grill in Birmingham, Ala. He has this sauce that — I don't even want to try to describe it." (The lobster is grilled).

Next, his mind leapt up north. "The meat course, let me have lamb sweetbreads from Daniel (in New York City). And, let's see, a hazelnut sorbet to clear the palate."

No meal would be complete without something sweet to finish it. "And then a simple creme brulee, completely traditional, and a napkin to clean up the blood after my nutritionist commits suicide. All these things I cannot eat now. I've got to eat crap like these salads."

The salads are working. He's lost weight. He's quick-witted. He's living life again, even if neuropathy slows his perambulation to an unsteady saunter.

"I am trying to get my health back. I came here from my trainer. I said, 'I need to be able to talk for a couple of hours after this meeting, so could you kill me less today?' She says, 'Mr. Pat, I hurt you because I love you.' Kind of like The Citadel plebes. She's making me do things I should not do, as a 90-year-old man I should not have to do any of this. But she does it anyway. When I came here, she said, 'Tell me what you will eat Mr. Pat.' I said, 'It's none of your business.' She said, 'Promise me you will not eat bad.' She'll be mad that I even gave you that menu, by the way."

It was arguably the most serious moment of the conversation, after which we talked about murder, poverty, racism, presidential politics, the detrimental influence of technology, gay marriage and novel writing, among other topics.

Birthday bash

Conroy, by the way, isn't 90; he was exaggerating. He does that. In fact, he's 70. And the University of South Carolina Press, which now employs him as a fiction editor in charge of the imprint Stony River Books, is throwing a big birthday bash for the crotchety old man this week in Beaufort.

"Pat Conroy at 70" is a three-day literary event featuring a slew of South Carolina heavy hitters and special guests from off. Presenters include editors Jonathan Galassi, Nan Talese and USC Press director

Jonathan Haupt; writers Marjory Wentworth, Catherine Seltzer, Ron Rash and Pam Durban; artists Jonathan Green and Jonathan Hannah; chef-historian Sallie Ann Robinson; actors Michael O'Keefe and David Keith; and the Conroy siblings.

Planned events include a tour of Daufuskie Island, panel discussions of various kinds, a screening of "The Great Santini," book signings, a poetry reading and more.

Conroy said he's sorry he agreed to this fiasco. His ego got inflated for a second and he figured he'd appreciate the accolades and attention. Then he stuck a pin in it.

But he's exaggerating again, of course. Closer to the truth: Conroy is a very nice person, generous to a fault. He finds it difficult to say no when good people ask him for things. So when Haupt, an editor Conroy admires (and works for), suggested a party, Conroy hummed and hawed, then agreed.

"Being celebrated comes as unnaturally to Conroy as fame and fortune," Haupt wrote in an email. "For him, these are the unexpected outcomes of his writing life, well-deserved and deeply appreciated in every regard, but unexpected nonetheless. So he was a bit resistant to the prospects of being honored with a festival that is at once for him and about him, but he also appreciated it for the gift that it is."

Conroy joked with his boss about banning Bernie Schein, a close Beaufort friend whose decades of private taunts and mockery have provided the essential antidote to all that public praise and adoration.

"His attempts to have Bernie Schein banned from the event seem to have failed, but I suppose we will at least honor his request that no one, most of all Bernie, sing 'Happy Birthday' to him," Haupt wrote.

The big party will begin, unofficially, with a private event in the backyard of the riverfront home Conroy shares with his wife, the writer Cassandra King. It will be his way of affirming people he loves and, at the same time, sticking a finger in the eye of the conservative politics he abhors. Conroy and King will host a gay wedding.

Party politics

"I am stunned that gay marriage is happening," he said. As soon as Conroy heard about the Supreme Court ruling that legalized gay marriage nationally, he called the brother of a good friend who's been in a committed relationship for nearly 30 years. "I called up and said, 'Why don't you get married in my yard?' They were celebrating, they were happy, and they said they'd do it. So the first thing that is going to set off my birthday weekend (which I would rather die than do, but I agreed to do it), they're thing is going to start off that weekend."

Conroy said he also couldn't believe he lived to see the election of a black president, but wasn't surprised about the backlash against Barack Obama, some of which is tinged with racism. "I expected *more* of a racist backlash, actually," he said.

Happy to talk about current affairs, he discussed the presidential campaign with a penchant for keen observations and injections of humor.

"There's something about Hillary Clinton being a woman president that would appeal to me a great deal," he said. Indeed, women probably should take over all of politics. "I regret Hillary Clinton is so difficult to love, I regret that. I'm sure that I'll vote for her. I wish that could be more a healing vote. I think that will be as polarizing as anything."

He said he admires Bernie Sanders ("I like him a ton") but worries about his electability. And the Republican field?

"I want somebody who seems presidential, and Trump does not seem presidential." Marco Rubio seems like a decent guy — except for his politics. And Jeb Bush seems decent, too, "although he does not seem alive in these debates. I don't know when the Bush genes come riveting to life, I don't know … who cranks the motor. So far it hasn't happened."

Conroy's primary political criteria are simple: "I realize I like somebody who seems not crazy."

His politics have been a point of contention throughout his life. During the period following the publication of "The Water is Wide," his memoir about teaching on Daufuskie Island in the late 1960s, he was "what passed for a Communist in South Carolina."

"I was called it so many times. And then the South sort of got accustomed to integration, I never thought they'd like it, but they got accustomed to it, and that faded."

What he really is, politically, is a Democrat. A Democrat in South Carolina. To other such outliers, he offered a word of advice: "Prepare for grotesque loneliness your entire life. Make lots of black friends."

For love of teaching

The man who was raised Catholic but believes a woman has the right to decide what happens to her body said he worries that the political and cultural gaps in the U.S. have widened to the point that bridging them has become nearly impossible.

He said public education suffers for two main reasons: the failure to properly educate poor blacks — and make up for the sins of slavery and Jim Crow — and the failure to treat teachers with the respect they deserve.

"The situation I fell into on Daufuskie Island, I think it's still there today. It shocks me."

The former teacher said he is suspicious of "school choice" policies that seem only to have exacerbated racial disparities.

"The charter movement is an attempt to save public schools by making them quasi-private," Conroy said. "When I hear 'charter schools' I hear 'white people.' "

And the obsession with testing has been a "disaster."

"It's made teaching the worst job in the country."

Public education would get a lot better if teachers were empowered and paid better and supported by parents rather than harassed all the time, he said.

"I met a teacher in Philadelphia. The inner city. I asked, 'How are your kids doing?' She says, 'They're failing, my schools failing, I'm failing, I'm about to get fired.' 'Why don't you quit?' 'Because I love those kids. They need me. I'm good for them.' I'm thinking, these are holy people. This is a kind of community of monks and nuns that you can't — I don't know how they afford houses and cars!"

If he hadn't become a writer, he'd have continued on a teaching track, Conroy said. Though it's unclear whether he could have circumvented the obstacles thrown up after the publication of "The Water is Wide." He was essentially blacklisted. Terrible "recommendation" letters piled up, as if someone was stacking the deck against him, determined to destroy all future teaching prospects, he said.

Four years later, he would be blacklisted again, after the publication of "The Great Santini," a novel that thinly disguised the dysfunction of his own family.

And four years after that, Conroy would be blacklisted yet again, this time from his alma mater, The Citadel, after the publication of "The Lords of Discipline."

It's as if the guy was looking for trouble. Or was he just an artist looking for Truth?

'Showing the world'

Truth revealed itself after the June 17 mass shooting at Emanuel AME Church. The murders were shocking, but Conroy was even more stunned by the instant forgiveness expressed by some of the victims' family members.

It was "a black church showing the world how it should act," he said.

"I still don't know how those people did that," Conroy marveled. "And then the reaction of the city of Charleston itself, and then the reaction of the country itself. I don't think Hollywood could have directed anything better to explain how the races should respond to each other. And that it came from Charleston was one of the great surprises and delights of my life. ... That church has become the new Selma bridge. It represents something now, bigger than it was, bigger than itself, and it's going to change for ever. I don't think they'll ever get that back."

Race is a subject he addresses in his new novel, tentatively titled "Storms of Aquarius." It's set in Charleston during the middle 1970s when the rebellion of the Age of Aquarius, or at least its misty aftereffects, reached the Lowcountry.

It was a time of radical change, of integration. The new novel shares the experiences of poor black families working for wealthy whites south of Broad Street. "Class is the basic theme of the book," Conroy said.

For the first time, he is writing a character who gets shipped to Vietnam.

"I had eight classmates die in Vietnam," The Citadel graduate said. "Four were kids who I loved. It was the defining moment of my generation."

He is writing the new book on yellow legal pads, as he always has done. Actual writing, in his immaculate script that no editor could possibly have trouble with. Conroy shuns technology. He is not a Luddite. "Even worse. I'm a Neanderthal."

"My children say, 'Dad, you'll be more connected.' I say, 'I want to be less connected.' In the world I live in, technology is not something that enhances that world. I told myself I'd commit suicide if I ever see myself looking at my phone in an airport." (He did recently acquire an iPhone.) "I was in the Charleston airport not long ago, and the whole airport was looking at their hands. No one was talking to each other, or if they were talking to each other they were still looking at the phone in their hand. ... My children go nuts if they send me messages on my Facebook page. I have never seen the Facebook page, I don't know who answers it."

Not long ago Conroy's granddaughter came to stay for a week. Her parents handed the child over and admonished Conroy and King: "Do not let her play video games!"

"We both nodded. The door shut. They went off. And I went back into her bedroom and said, 'Excuse me Alessandra, are you playing a video game right now?' 'Of course.' 'Did you hear what your dad said?' 'Yes I did. But you're my grandparents and you'll let me do anything I want because you love me so much. I've been looking forward to playing these video games ever since we flew in from Texas.' I don't think we saw her for five days."

Yet Conroy fretted over his promise.

"Should we say anything?" he asked his wife.

"She seems so happy Pat," King replied.

Grandparenting

Parenting is something Conroy has often worried about, probably because of the trauma he endured during his own childhood. His father was abusive; his mother was an enabler. Conroy, the oldest of seven siblings, felt obligated to protect his brothers and sisters, sometimes inserting himself between his father's fist and his family's flesh.

"My one rule with my daughters: I said, 'Girls, I'm not going to be one of those fathers who interferes, you're not going to hear much from me at all. But I'd like you to promise me one thing, you'll try to date guys that I don't absolutely hate. If you'll just do that for me I'd appreciate it.' Of course not one of them kept that rule."

Two are teachers, one is an artist, one puts out a newsletter for Emory University Medical Center.

"They're all doing well," Conroy said. "It's an accident."

Now he worries about his grandchildren, who range in age from 7 to 21.

"I always tell my grandchildren, 'I don't like grandchildren, I'm very different from most people. You read about bear-like grandfathers in children's books. I'm not like that. I'm a foul-tempered grandfather, and I want you all to keep away from me as much as possible.' And they completely ignore me."

Here's a typical scene:

"Poppy are you writing?"

"Yes I am."

"Do you want us to come in?"

"No, I want you to get out of here." (They come in.)

"Did you hear me say I'm writing?"

"Yes we did."

But what is a doting grandfather to do? Resistance is futile.

"It's life," Conroy said. "It comes by you."

How Polly Sheppard, a Survivor of the Emanuel Mass Shooting, Carries On

It doesn't take long before the first embrace. And then Polly Sheppard greets another of the students, then another.

This group of young evangelicals, affiliated with the parachurch ministry Cru, is here at Emanuel AME Church to learn more about the 2015 mass shooting, visit the sanctuary and offer their prayers. They have just watched Brian Tetsuro Ivie's documentary "Emanuel," and they recognize Sheppard, who is visiting the church grounds, where a memorial soon will be erected.

The exchange between this survivor of the attack and the Cru crew is polite, warm, engaging.

Because that's how the magnanimous Sheppard operates. Mostly, she sees the good in people. She's ready with a smile.

She witnessed round after round of bullets from a handgun strike her friends and colleagues again and again and watched as their blood darkened the beige tile floor of the basement room where Bible studies were held. She faced down a racist killer. She survived a massacre.

Her faith and her inner strength — the strength of a mother of four boys, the strength of an experienced nurse, the strength of a Black woman from Florence — has not wavered much.

Others surely would have been transformed by such trauma, their courage compromised, their view of the world cast in shadow, their faith in humanity shattered. Others would have turned inward to cope with their swirling demons.

Not Miss Polly.

Promise of serenity

Today, she is focused on the memorial, and points to where the Fellowship Benches will go, where the Names Fountain will be positioned, where the asphalt lot will be transformed into a green Survivors' Garden. Each of the survivors — Sheppard; Felicia Sanders and her granddaughter; Jennifer Pinckney and her daughter — will have a live oak tree planted in their honor. The garden will include six benches on which visitors can contemplate how a scorched earth eventually turns green again.

Sheppard is an active member of the committee set up by a nonprofit called the Mother Emanuel Memorial Foundation, which is independent of the church and overseeing the project. She might never be able to find the serenity promised by the memorial, though, not if she keeps hearing about mass shootings.

The recent attacks in Buffalo and Uvalde, Texas, pain her in ways few can comprehend. She knows what it's like to hide under a desk, to relinquish herself to the certainty of imminent violence. She knows what it's like to look a killer in the eyes, to recite the 23rd Psalm loud enough so he can hear the words. She knows what it's like to feel for an absent pulse.

So Polly Sheppard speaks out in favor of gun regulation and a hate crimes bill, and she struggles to understand why it's so difficult to pass laws that would save lives.

If you find a dead fish in its aquarium, she said, and before long you notice other dead fish, it becomes evident that the water is the problem.

"So change the water."

In front of your eyes

Sheppard, 77, avoids the press now. After the May 14 mass shooting by a hate-filled White teenager at a Tops store in Buffalo, reporters called her for comment. She wouldn't answer. Too painful. Too chronic.

She hates making public appearances, too. Especially if she's expected to adhere to a script. "Most of the time I just talk," she said. A Q&A format is best. That way, she can answer freely. She will speak her mind.

Lately, she's been thinking about the infection that corrupts our body politic — how violence has been, is still, wielded against African Americans, how unresolved racial animus festers.

She offers a proposal: 100 Black people in each major U.S. city should go en masse to the gun store to buy AR-15s. Then see what happens.

A retired jail nurse accustomed to treating wounds to the flesh, she was mostly blind to the infection that penetrated deep into national psyche. But then a white supremacist in love with the Confederate battle flag and armed with a Glock .45, told Sheppard he would let her live to tell the story.

So she tells the story about America's sickness, about the social and political systems that resist good-faith efforts to change them. She reminds others of the promises broken and opportunities denied over the course of history, and of injustices that persist today.

"I didn't see these systems," she said. "They were right in front of your eyes, but you don't see them."

The violence has its origins, and its consequences.

Hollow-point bullets, she said, cause a devastating wound.

The shadow of death

Just before Bible study on June 17, 2015, Emanuel AME Church was full of people attending an annual conference, and Sheppard was there to help. She sat on Emanuel's stewardship and finance committee. She was invested in her church. She often lent a helping hand.

She attended the insurance meeting, then the budget meeting. She was there all day. She planned to skip the Bible study. But in the bathroom, her best friend Myra Thompson, who had just been ordained and was about to lead her first Wednesday night session, challenged her. You should stay, that's what friends do, Thompson told her with a wink.

"She kept her eyes on me so I couldn't sneak out," Sheppard recalls.

When the gunshots began to pop, Sheppard first assumed it was faulty wiring in the building. Then came the shouts, the agony. She hid under a table by the kitchen at the back of the Fellowship Hall.

Dylann Roof killed the Rev. Clementa Pinckney first, then shot the Rev. Daniel Simmons, who had rushed to assist his pastor.

"He kept shooting," Sheppard said. "I could hear the clips falling."

From under the table, she called 911, then watched his feet as he approached.

The Lord is my shepherd; I shall not want. He maketh me to lie down in green pastures: he leadeth me beside the still waters. ...

"I had given up," she said. "My body was loose. I was just waiting for the bullet."

Yea, though I walk through the valley of the shadow of death, I will fear no evil: for thou art with me …

When he reached Sheppard, the killer stopped.

"Did I shoot you yet?"

"No."

"I'm not going to."

After he left, she scrambled to assist the wounded. Most already were dead.

Get rid of the hatred

It helps her to talk about it sometimes. It keeps the details fresh, it allows her to release built-up pressure, it gives her courage.

"You find you have strength," she said. "I don't know where it comes from."

She didn't forgive the killer right away, but eventually she found the will to do so. Not for his sake, but for her own.

"You've got to get rid of the hatred to move forward," she said.

Three years of counseling from the Medical University of South Carolina's Connie Best helped immensely. So did her remaining friendships. She had lost Thompson, and other close friends, Sharonda Singleton and Ethel Lance. She had lost her beloved pastor. She had lost her sense of belonging at Mother Emanuel.

But she still had Felicia Sanders, who protected her granddaughter and survived the assault by playing dead.

And she had her faith, everlasting.

Sheppard and Sanders met at Emanuel in the 1990s. They attended Sunday School together. They shared a similar devotion to their church and often dug into their own pockets to help pay for this or that.

"I always admired her style," Sanders said of her friend. "Her demeanor is always calm. She's a go-getter. If anything needed to be done, she does it. She doesn't tolerate a lot of craziness."

Both women insist on living their lives on their terms. They lean on one another. They protect one another.

"The only person who understands both of us is both of us," Sheppard said.

A church fund started soon after the mass shooting, and an $88 million settlement with the federal government last year provided families of the nine victims and survivors of the attack with some money. Sheppard started the Polly Sheppard Foundation in partnership with Trident Technical College to give scholarships to students who want to become nurses serving in detention centers and prisons, like she did.

Sanders started the Tywanza Sanders Legacy Foundation, named for her son who tried to protect the others from Roof's racist rage, including Sheppard and his aunt Susie Jackson. The foundation awards several academic and trade school scholarships a year.

Uncommon strength

Born in Florence in 1944, Polly Daniels worked part time in the cotton fields while she was in school. After graduation, she found a job with a motor company soldering parts. She's got the burn scars to prove it. When the company moved abroad, she used the severance money to go back to school and become a licensed practical nurse.

She married at 19 and had four boys, then divorced after seven years when it became apparent the marriage was untenable. She took her kids to The Bronx so she could make more money and find them better schools, she said.

In 1980, she returned to South Carolina, where a friend soon introduced her to James Sheppard, a Charleston native. They settled in the Lowcountry and joined Mother Emanuel.

Since the shootings, though, they have been active members of Mt. Zion AME Church. The Rev. Kylon Middleton, who was pastoring a church in Georgetown in 2015, rushed to Charleston when he heard about the attack. Pinckney was a close friend, and Middleton would provide essential support to his family in the aftermath. He got to know Sheppard in those first few days, and the two of them bonded.

That November, Middleton was transferred to Mt. Zion, and the Sheppards immediately became active participants, helping with Sunday School, Bible study and other activities of their new congregation.

She's no Bible thumper, but she's a vocal and engaged proponent of her faith, Middleton said.

"She provides context," he said. "She edifies the body of Christ through her lived experience as a Christian."

When Middleton tries to imagine the unimaginable — how Sheppard managed the violence, how she found her path forward — he marvels at her uncommon strength.

"You could imagine something this horrific could cause a person to withdraw, but she has pushed right on in," he said.

In the Fellowship Hall, as Roof brandished his gun before her, she recited a sacred text proclaiming God's greatness.

"She was shouting it out," he said.

She was providing the assailant with words of God's grace and power.

"Surely, goodness and mercy shall follow her all the days of her life," he said, quoting the psalm.

Finding a path forward

When Margaret Seidler was involved in creating a memorial for the Charleston International Airport, she consulted with Sheppard. Soon they strengthened their connection as Seidler helped lead the Illumination Project with the Charleston Police Department.

"I just kept realizing that she was teaching me a strength and a courage that I've never seen," Seidler said. "She cannot accept the status quo, and she is willing to put herself out front to find a path forward."

As Sheppard enlightened her friend, Seidler grew determined to provide unconditional support. She helped Sheppard prepare for her appearance at the Democratic National Convention. She helped get the foundation set up. She traveled with Sheppard to civil rights history sites in Alabama and Georgia.

"Polly bolsters me," she said. "If I start to lose hope, she's there for me. She points her right index finger up at the sky and says, 'The Lord is going to take care of this.' She is quite a light, a bright shining light, and thank God for her."

After the shooting, Sheppard decided to allow her son Oscar, a hairstylist, to give her a new look. She donned sunglasses. She wanted to be incognito. But James and her four children, her family in Florence, and her friends old and new made it easy for her to find her footing.

Seven years after Roof tried to start a race war by firing 77 bullets in a sacred space, and more than five years after he was tried for federal hate crimes and sentenced to death, Polly Sheppard has settled into a routine. She gets up late, eats breakfast, reads the newspaper, including the obituary section, does a little housework, reads a good novel or a book about American history, then maybe visits an antique shop. She doesn't much like cooking anymore. She takes a moment to think before she opens her mouth to say something.

She prefers a chat with a friend, a visit to Mt. Zion, a meeting about the memorial. Sometimes a day or two will pass and she'll realize she didn't think about the strange young man at the Bible study. Sometimes she'll linger at the antique stores and James will worry, or she'll get a call from her youngest son Gilbert. "Where you at, lady?" he'll ask, concerned like his stepfather. Soon, she and James will be back in Florence for good, closer to her extended family.

Sheppard's well-earned skepticism about the motivation of others has hardened a little since 2015, but then there are those encounters that quickly assuage her doubts. A call from Sanders or Seidler. A good word at church. Or an encounter with earnest students visiting Mother Emanuel, seeking to understand the origins of hate and the source of grace.

That's what provokes a smile.

That's what elicits her embrace.

IV.

THE ARTISTIC IMPULSE:
Confronting Human Nature

Introduction
by Mark Sloan

Arriving in Charleston in 1994 to be the new Director of the College of Charleston's "Halsey Gallery" as it was then known, I asked an obvious question to members of the arts community: "What is the status of arts writing in this area?" I was to learn that the only art "critic" in the city wrote for The Post and Courier, and was legally blind (R.I.P. Nicholas Drake). When I told this to one of my NYC art colleagues, she said, snarkily, "Well, maybe we all get what we deserve."

Fast forward to 2004 and the arrival of Adam Parker. Adam is much more than a reviewer, and he is not really a critic, as such. He is a thinker — a poser of big questions — a catalyst. I was thrilled when he first started writing for the paper because first of all, he is a gifted writer. Secondly, he has a penchant for getting at the heart of the matter, no matter the subject. This is his superpower. I found myself reading his articles each week because I was interested to see what caught his attention, and I always learned something (usually many things) that surprised me.

Parker has an inquisitive mind and an uncanny ability to draw connections between seemingly disparate data points. His is a "lively" intellect; one that probes for the larger narratives beneath the ostensible subject. Story after story he has demonstrated his capacity for aggregating information, synthesizing its component parts, and presenting it in such a compelling way that offers readers threads to follow on their own, should they be so inclined. Like all of the best writers, Parker propels us to ask more questions than he answers.

My favorite thing about Adam Parker's writing is that he assumes as certain level of cultural intelligence of his reader. He is never pedantic or preachy, and he never talks "down" to his readers. Rather, he presents the stories in such a way as to draw us in, to make us a part of his discoveries. We invariably want to know more, now that we have Parker's take on the subject. In this way, he has served a vital function within our larger community. He has given breath to so many ideas and issues, and his writing is provocative in the sense that he gets tongues wagging. He posits notions that beg for a response. His is not a passive voice, but a well-informed, passionate, and inquisitive one — not afraid to jump into the fray.

It must be said also, that his interests are capacious and expansive. He is equally at home discussing opera, film, visual art, cigars, sailboats, rock 'n' roll, or literature (to list but a few of his enthusiasms), and he is an astute student of history and politics — all of which he brings to his writing. His self-assigned mission seems to be to illuminate big ideas and provide the impetus for understanding the implications of them — a true gift for his readers.

Mark Sloan was director and chief curator of the Halsey Institute of Contemporary Art at the College of Charleston. Now he is a consultant based in Chapel Hill, N.C.

The Quandary of Alice Ravenel Huger Smith

Plantation series by watercolorist soothes the eye, raises questions

It's unusual to see all 29 of these gorgeous watercolors by Alice Ravenel Huger Smith hanging together in one space. They rarely leave their sequestered storage of the Gibbes Museum, for they are sensitive to light and must be protected.

In recent years, the museum has worked with the Strauss Center at Harvard University to restore them, removing the threat of acid backings among other measures taken, an effort that has markedly improved both the appearance and prospect for long-term survival of these remarkable pictures.

Now through July 16, museum visitors can see the entirety of Smith's famed "Carolina Rice Plantation of the Fifties" series.

The premier artist of the Charleston Renaissance, Smith sought in the middle 1930s to document a dead age. Hers was the last generation that would be able to cull from memories of plantation life in the antebellum South, and she took it upon herself to preserve that period in a series of nostalgic images that would be accompanied by her father's memoirs and an essay on rice cultivation by the historian Herbert Ravenel Sass.

Those who stand before these watercolors cannot help but be impressed by their loveliness, and many say so when visiting the Gibbes, according to its curators and ticket takers.

Smith was a master manipulator of watercolor, creating images, landscapes mostly, influenced by Japanese printmaking and woodblocks and romantic English art that transformed the objects of nature into symbol, myth and memory.

Interestingly, her skillful use of color, portrayal of natural light and expressive brushwork was little influenced by French Impressionism, which had taken the art world by storm in the latter half of the 19th century when Smith was first learning how to paint.

She was mostly self-taught, prone to homesickness and avoided travel abroad, Martha Severens writes in her illustrated biography of the artist, "Alice Ravenel Huger Smith."

She made these plantation paintings during the height of Jim Crow, when black people in Charleston and throughout the country were subjected to humiliating discrimination and life-threatening abuse.

She knew of this, of course. She lived downtown, a single woman surviving on the income generated from the sale of her art. Not far away from her was intense poverty. This was the period of "Porgy and Bess," of street calls and street fights, of hunger and vocal prayer.

Charleston was a city in limbo, its glorious wealth of the rice years diminished, its economic revival still decades away. The disquiet of her times likely provoked in her a strong sense of "longing for things to be as they were," noted Gibbes Executive Director Angela Mack.

"Things as they were" meant relative calm and order, a historic period when blacks knew their place and white planters were firmly in charge, when life for the privileged class was simple and wealth abundant.

"Yes, times do change," Smith wrote at the beginning of her "Reminiscences," an autobiography she produced in about 1950. "Small places and big places alike show it. Perhaps small happenings show it as sharply as great events, and one looks with surprise at the differences that one never noticed during the endless moments of what might be called trivial evolution."

The watercolors reflect well her sense of change, and her profound nostalgia, said College of Charleston historian and archivist Harlan Greene.

"Even at the time, she had created a beautiful fantasy of the past," Greene said. "I think people really want to believe 'if only': If only the past was that lovely, that pastel."

Her interpretations of plantation life also likely were more marketable than images of reality, Mack said.

When Winslow Homer created his 1876 canvas called "A Visit From the Old Mistress," some observers didn't quite know what to make of it. It was one of very few pictures that portrayed blacks and whites together (in this case, freed slaves living in a ramshackle cabin and the former mistress of the big house who, until recently, owned them). It represented a scene from the present, an inevitable awkwardness.

"In creating a canvas shared by black and white people (Homer) left the critics confused about what to look at, and frustrated that answers (and perhaps more precisely authority) were not found in the face of physicality of the mistress," wrote Alexis Boylan in her essay "From Gilded Age to 'Gone with the Wind,'" collected in the volume "Landscape of Slavery."

Smith, too, portrayed blacks and whites together, but hers were pastoral scenes of the past, and the social hierarchy was explicit.

In one watercolor (the first of her series), called "Sunday Morning at the Great House," smiling slaves and their children line up to pay their respects to the master and mistress, with the rector and his wife looking on from the first-floor piazza. It's an orderly and idealized scene, washed clean of the ugliness of slavery.

When she paints slaves at work, they are figures — mere shapes and gestures, really — that extend from or blend in with the landscape. Toil, sweat, disease and distress are invisible. Instead, the viewer is left to marvel at Smith's delicate brush strokes evoking the Lowcountry's warm light, golden rice fields and blue waterways.

Gibbes curator Sara Arnold said the artist was not only expressing nostalgia for a bygone era, she was creating pictures that purposefully soothed rather than riled the viewer.

"It was also a way to restore order," Arnold said, adding that slavery *per se* was not really Smith's primary subject. She was more interested in landscape, and the ways in which it could communicate a sense of place and identity.

Smith was generally resistant to change, Arnold said. She hated the automobile. She loved to take walks.

With a genetic stake in prominent Charleston families, she was also acutely aware of her exceptional lineage. To be invited to dinner at the Smith home was to have reached the upper echelons of Charleston society, noted Mack.

But that resistance was measured. In her "Reminiscences" she wrote of her divided allegiance: "I was brought up on the heels of a struggle for personal and sectional liberty and I naturally grew to admire the generation before me. Broken in body with the iron of great despair in their soul, they were brave enough to face the ruins and build again. I have lived beyond that period and I am eager to follow a new generation in its progress, but my allegiance is divided, first to the old, then to the new. It is useless to try and relive the past just as it is unnecessary to discard everything that came before us."

Smith's dreamy landscapes were mostly imagined, Arnold said, but in the years before World War II, local plantations still were places where crops were cultivated and laborers plowed the soil, so it's likely that she drew some inspiration from real life.

She donated her "Rice Plantation" series to the Carolina Art Association in 1936, ensuring the set would remain intact and cared for. Many other works she sold and, over the years since her death in 1958, Smith has won admirers near and far.

The complete series displayed now at the Gibbes showcases the extraordinary work and gives viewers an opportunity to consider it in a new light. The impact of the whole set is quite different from the effect wrought by one or two of the pictures. The context is clearer, the beauty multiplied, the artistic quandary rendered more acute.

Arnold said it's the Gibbes' responsibility and privilege to share these works and to present them as honestly as possible. "They are beautiful, but they ignore the real story of the antebellum plantation," she said.

Are their distortions of history to be overlooked? Do we limit ourselves to admiring their elegance and grace? Does the series cross the line between art and propaganda?

"Hopefully people will ask those questions," Arnold said.

Confronting Nature and Time

Two McClellanville artists find their place

Each maneuver of the tiny knife leaves an elegant groove in the hard boxwood block. As he adds line after line, the image, reversed, emerges. A figure on a moonlit sea or a crowd under an infernal sky, or the disembodied hands of an old man.

He spreads the ink and places a piece of paper atop the block of wood in the century-old iron-hand press, then pulls the large lever.

This is slow, lonely work, and John McWilliams becomes lost in his thoughts and in the art-making process. This is his comfort zone, this McClellanville studio, a place of daily ritual and contemplation, of music and coffee and memory.

On the other side of the studio, Nancy Marshall makes her photographs, lost in her own thoughts, navigating a magical world she shares in part with her husband. The two of them are at home here, content to be among the splayed oaks and tidal creeks, the mosquitoes and oyster catchers, a few good friends.

This bucolic village and the surrounding area in the northern reaches of Charleston County is home to a disproportionate number of artists, writers and professionals, several of whom settled here in the 1970s, happy to find a quiet, picturesque place to raise their children. They are the "come-heres" who have joined the "been-heres" or "stay-puts" — the fishermen and their families. A few live in town; others a few miles away along the water or in the woods.

McWilliams and Marshall first came here because of a famous photograph. He saw Robert Frank's image of the village barbershop, its empty chair and hair products visible through the screen door. The photograph, dated 1955, was part of Frank's collection, "The Americans," and it captured the imagination of McWilliams who, at the time, was teaching art at Georgia State University, taking his own remarkable photographs and seeking a quiet country retreat from the bustle of Atlanta.

He knew nothing of McClellanville but sought it out in the early 1970s because of that barbershop.

"It was like I had driven into a time warp," he said.

A student, Willy Filmore, who grew up in St. Stephens, was friends with a couple who had moved to the McClellanville. He arranged for McWilliams to meet Jim and Patty Fulcher. Jim was the only family physician working in the remote town. The two men hit it off.

"Jim and I had this love for creeks and marshes," McWilliams said.

Soon, the teacher-photographer met his future mate, Marshall, at Georgia State, and the couple made regular treks to the Lowcountry creeks, forging and strengthening their friendship with the Fulchers.

McWilliams, who is the nephew of Julia Child and a Massachusetts native, had two children from a previous marriage. Together they had two more. The pair quickly met other like-minded people — Ted and Dale Rosengarten, Billy Baldwin, Susan Williams, Stephanie Waldron, Tommy and Sarah Graham, Bill and Lanie Youngman — all satisfied in their own way with McClellanville's isolation and its vulnerability to nature.

McWilliams and Marshall bought some property in the early 1980s and first built a cabin, later a house. When he retired from Georgia State in 2004, the couple moved east to the coast to stay. For him, photography gave way to print-making (though he continued to draw). For both, the Lowcountry was a melancholy land of never-ending discovery.

McWilliams carves his lines and presses his blocks of wood against the paper. The mechanics satisfy him; the resulting image pleases us. Marshall, instead, makes the process part of the final product. We look at her singular images, whether portraits or landscapes, and we see not only the image but all that went into producing it: the choice of camera, the framing of the composition, the exposure, the application of chemicals, the texture and temper of the paper.

He makes stark pictures that startle the eye and, at the same time, offer a glimpse into his subconscious where McWilliams confronts his demons and unleashes his fantasies. She makes pictures that caress the eye and encourage scrutiny. Both make emotionally charged work, but the power source is as different as could be.

'What was there'

"They are both great artists, each in his and her own way," said Dale Rosengarten, director of the Jewish Heritage Collection at the College of Charleston Library. "They are what I would call world-class artists. They would stand out anywhere."

Close friends, the Rosengartens and the two artists often socialize, swim in the creek, bicycle around town and practice a little yoga together.

"I admire the way they operate," Dale Rosengarten said. "Every morning, even weekends, they go to their studios, work all day long on their art."

In 1975, McWilliams received a National Endowment for the Arts photography fellowship, and in 1977, he landed a coveted Guggenheim Fellowship. This enabled him to pursue an ambitious project that culminated with the publication of a book, "Land of Deepest Shade: Photographs of the South by John McWilliams." His friend Ted Rosengarten, author of the National Book Award-winning "All God's Dangers: The Life of Nate Shaw," wrote the introduction.

The black-and-white images portray a ravaged landscape. They are distillations of Southern decay. His favorite photo, the once gracing the cover, shows an old tree smothered by cotton waste.

"It's a photography of absence, a photography of ruins, a photography that begs you to think about what was there," Rosengarten said.

Marshall has been taking pictures of the Southern landscape, too. In 1980, she shot a series of smoky pictures on Ossabaw Island near Savannah that reveal her fascination with time and place and her habit of juxtaposing that which is human (or human-made) with nature.

In 2007 and 2008, she traveled to Andalusia farm near Milledgeville, Ga., in her home state, to photograph the homestead where Flannery O'Connor spent her last 13 years. The images are simple, but in them one senses the ghost of O'Connor.

Soon after, she teamed with her husband on a series of color photographs of African-American car club members in Charleston County, published in the magazine Southern Spaces in 2010. The pictures, taken in McClellanville, show proud car owners standing by their vehicles and offer a glimpse into a Lowcountry cultural phenomenon few know about. These bold photographs of posed figures and shiny automobiles do much to humanize their subjects.

In 2015, Marshall shot a series of myth-like portraits of a young woman, Pier Louise, among the trees and foliage, blurring the line between subject and setting. And there have been many other projects — of battlefields, of rivers and ruins, of Hampton Plantation — each relying on a particular technique (wet plate, platinum and palladium printing) and set of equipment (panoramic, large-format, pin-hole).

Processing grief

In 2012, after years battling opioid addiction, McWilliams' son J.J. died.

"Some people are just wired to not be able to handle life," he said. "He was a complex person, he had a beautiful reality about him."

J.J. had moved to McClellanville from Portland, Ore., to recover, to fish on the marsh, to find happiness. And he did, for a while. McWilliams struggled to process his death, relying on art to explore his feelings about fatherhood, its joys and burdens. The Halsey Institute of Contemporary Art collaborated with Horse & Buggy Press to produce a special limited edition of "Sons & Father," a small-format volume featuring McWilliams' woodcut prints.

The book was an ancillary product of a 2016 exhibit at the Halsey called "Prophesies," an important showcase of the work of the famously modest artist.

"I first learned of John McWilliams back in 1989 when his book 'Land of Deepest Shade' came out," Sloan said. "I heard him give an artist talk at a national conference in the early 1990s, at which he showed images and told the story of building his own boat and sailing it to Bermuda. The story was riveting, and the images incredibly moving."

Sloan marveled as McWilliams developed his printing style.

"I see him very much in the tradition of William Blake," he said. "His works are singularly dark and foreboding. They are allegorical in their meaning. Another strong component in his work is the narrative arc. In this way, he is something of an acolyte of Lynd Ward, the graphic novelist of the 1930s. I see that both his photography and printmaking share a certain affinity for the transformative power of nature. Nature is often pitted against human nature in John's compositions. Are we are part of, or apart from nature, he seems to be asking."

Jim Fulcher remembers that sail to Bermuda on the sloop built by McWilliams after a Chuck Payne design. It was just the two of them, eight days there, 12 days back. They were becalmed for a two or three days on the return, so they took an inventory of the food and drink on board and were reassured.

"When he gets on a passion, he's got focus," Fulcher said, referring as much to his friend's love for the sea as his commitment to his art.

The confrontation

Living and working, drawing and fishing, printing and swimming. It's all part of a singular experience, each activity informing the others.

"It's extremely important to have a process," McWilliams said. It's his way of making sense of the world. And he's glad for the occasional exhibition, which provides feedback and offers him a chance to have a fresh look at his work, to take inventory of it, to recognize patterns and themes.

Sometimes he will get a commission, though the money it brings is never the priority. In the past, McWilliams would do some photographic survey and documentary work to record obsolete technology before it disappeared forever.

Once he was asked to photograph an abandoned steel mill. "It was like an archaeological thing," he said, so dark inside he opened his camera shutter then set off a series of huge flash bulbs along each wall of the cavernous space. The result was a fully lit image of decay.

Decay is a specialty of both artists, whose photographs often set in contrast the impermanence of human endeavor and the inexorable force of nature.

In their studio, the artists seem all too aware of that confrontation. One sees the exertions and endurance, but also the fugitive moment. That is why they work, slowly producing image after image, pictures that frame an idea and fix time. It is what they know to do.

"I work all the time because really it's the thing that anchors me," McWilliams said. "Doing my art has saved my life many times."

'One-Man Preservation Army'

Ronald Ramsey captures memories of
Charleston's changing cityscape

It's difficult at first to know what to make of it all. Ronald Wayne Ramsey is not your typical artist and not your typical preservationist.

Yet Ramsey, a small fellow with a round head, thinning hair, a big smile and a way of talking that can be hard to understand, has been obsessively documenting old Charleston buildings for decades, creating intricate drawings, collecting objects from the sites and assembling newspaper clippings and other written records of what has transpired within the city's landscape.

When all this material was brought to the attention of Mark Sloan, director of the Halsey Institute for Contemporary Art at the College of Charleston, he didn't quite know what he should do with it. When nearly two years ago he asked Ramsey's friends and advocates at Hines Studios on upper King Street to display some of Ramsey's vast collection of stuff in the shop so that it might be contemplated better, Sloan began to see the possibilities.

"Ahead of the Wrecking Ball: Ronald Ramsey and the Preservation of Charleston" opens Saturday at the Halsey in the smaller of the two galleries. It includes numerous finely etched drawings, fascinating remnants, notebooks brimming with Ramsey's research, a short documentary by artist-filmmaker David Boatwright and more.

Looking at the work, it becomes clear what Ramsey is doing. He is telling a story, the extended story of our city. For about 40 years, he has methodically recorded the decaying parts of town. In so doing, Ramsey has discovered fascinating details of what life was like once upon a time. He has been able to piece together a portrait of constantly changing urban terrain.

Buildings tell stories

In the private shop of Hines Studios in the Neck Area of the peninsula, past the tattoo parlors and the Kingdom Hall, Ramsey and Jason Petitpain stand chatting about the Charleston of yore. Ramsey recalls the story of the Six Mile Wayfarer House, which once stood where a Kangaroo gas station now is found. In the 19th century, this area was far outside the confines of the city. Travelers would stop for a meal, a hot cup of tea and a night's rest. The proprietors, John and Lavinia Fisher, were gangsters with sinister intentions.

The tea was laced with a drug. The bed was rigged to drop its inhabitant through the floor and (perhaps) upon several erect spikes. Possessions were transferred from the newly dead to the nefarious Fishers.

Eventually they were caught and hung, leaving only a remarkable legend for future generations to muse over.

Such stories seem to provide the fuel that keeps Ramsey prowling the streets. Ordinary folk walk along Charleston's cobblestones and alleys and see what's there. Not Ramsey. He sees the ghosts of the past.

He was born Oct. 16, 1954, in downtown Charleston. His father was a property inspector for the health department and a watch repairman. Ramsey lived with his mother until her death, then moved moved to Joseph Floyd Manor in 1999.

He began drawing buildings in the late 1960s. The artistic impulse came first, he said. Only later did he develop an interest in preservation.

Currently, he's concerned about the facade of the Bennett Rice Mill, standing precariously at an entrance to the cruise ship terminal. It must be restored, then joined to the new terminal structure eventually to be built, he said. The new must not erase the old; it must pay its respects, it must recall what came before. Otherwise, what happens to Charleston?

Ramsey also is turning his eye toward a century-old house in North Charleston, one among a number of "nice old houses that need to be preserved for future generations," he said. And he's scrutinizing a former dime store on Reynolds Avenue and the former Charleston Naval Hospital on Rivers Avenue.

He thinks he's made drawings of at least 100 buildings so far.

Hoarders and friends

Petitpain, his brother David and their colleague Bob Hines have known Ramsey for at least a dozen years now. The artist-preservationist would wander into the old shop on King Street just south of Cannon Street with the latest drawing, or a few objects he gathered from a demolition site, and offer them for sale. The three glassworkers would happily open their wallets.

Over the years, they got to know Ramsey better, helping him find storage space for a growing collection of curios, introducing him to others captivated by the pearls found within the detritus of the city and the history that constantly threatened to escape one's grasp forever.

When Ramsey became fascinated with a table lodged in a home on Tracy Street, whose owner had bigger things to think about than the fate of old furniture and little patience for Ramsey's desires, the collector turned to the more direct and dogmatic approach of Jason Petitpain. It had been two years of intense longing on Ramsey's part, and when Petitpain showed up at the house he got an earful from the owner, too. Somehow, he got the table, escaping with it quickly as barbed epithets were flung from the doorway.

Anything for a friend.

"You know, we're all hoarders," Petitpain said, expressing sympathy for Ramsey. "We developed a relationship like that."

Ramsey sold his first drawing to David Petitpain, who thought it would make a fine birthday present for his brother.

"We were just blown away by these drawings," Jason Petitpain said. And they were blown away by the old signs and doorknobs and iron ornamentation and oversized hardware Ramsey lugged to the shop. This stuff was impossible to resist.

"I went to his apartment once, a cave full of incredible relics," Petitpain said. It's a small apartment in public housing, and the management hasn't entirely appreciated the significance of the relics that fill the room. "He's got to move stuff off his bed to go to sleep," Petitpain said.

So some years ago Petitpain helped him get a little organized, transported some of the ceramic pigs, glass plates, old fire alarm covers, faded signage and reams of documentation to a storage space and to corners of Hines Studios.

That's when Petitpain got to know Ramsey better. That's when he began to understand what motivates the collector.

Six years ago, Petitpain became a personal trainer. He uses the money he earns to buy Ramsey's drawings.

'This amazing person'

When Sloan broached the idea of mounting a show devoted to Ramsey's work, the chief preservation officer of Historic Charleston Foundation felt a little inadequate.

"I had never heard of him when Mark started taking about this guy Ronald Wayne Ramsey, this incredible preservationist," Winslow Hastie said. "I was in the dark. What's wrong with me that I don't know this amazing person?"

Hastie queried colleagues and soon learned that Ramsey was no stranger to the foundation. He used to show up unannounced, often with a bag of stuff and some drawings that he'd give to Jonathan Poston, a preservation officer who left the organization in 2005.

"He develops relationships with people who he trusts, and who understand what he's trying to do," Hastie said. "I think he was misunderstood by a lot of people. He would call and be persistent. Some people probably considered him a nuisance."

At first glance, Ramsey's drawings have a childlike quality — until you scrutinize them and recognize the detail and accuracy.

"His process is still a mystery," Hastie said. "It almost doesn't matter, but it does make you think. How does he do it?"

What's more he understands intuitively that documentation is the first step in the preservation process, Hastie added. Without that, there can be no effective research of the social history.

"He's looking at vernacular structures that really didn't get a lot of notice until the late 1980s," Hastie said. Old Charleston businesses such as Swan Laundry or G.W. Aimar & Co. or the Woolfe Street ice house. "He's looking at these things that are not being appreciated and understanding that they are under threat because of that. That to me is the coolest."

And he's doing this from outside the preservation establishment, Hastie added.

"Preservation perhaps got overly focused on the physical structure and not on paying as much attention to the people, the social history of the site. In a way he's humanizing these buildings. You have to do that when fighting to save a structure."

An abiding love

Sloan called Ramsey Charleston's "best-kept secret."

"I'm really honored that the Halsey is the one to present his work to the public for the first time," Sloan said. "He's someone you'd see on the street looking down, his attention focused elsewhere, and you wouldn't expect he's a one-man preservation army. The packaging is very deceiving."

Ramsey has made some of what Sloan called "Imagination drawings" — of buildings that don't actually exist. This hints at Ramsey's artistic inclinations and his peculiar obsessions with the built environment.

"He has an uncanny spatial sense," an ability to see clearly in three dimensions and translate his subjects accurately into two dimensions, Sloan said. "And he has an abiding love for the architecture of this city, and its heritage. When he sees an old building slated to be destroyed, it's almost like the loss of a limb. Every chipping away at it is a diminishment."

Sloan is accustomed to working with lesser-known artists who work along the fringes — or entirely outside — of the established art world. He's an enthusiastic devotee of the unconventional. But even Sloan is a bit astonished by the Ramsey phenomenon.

Ramsey is nothing if not unconventional, a man devoted to his city who has created a significant body of work that leaves admiring scholars, artists and preservationists scratching their heads, wondering what to make of it all.

And that's just how Sloan likes it.

"Of all the things someone can spend time doing ... he has chosen to do this thing that's kind of epic in scope," Sloan said.

The Great Curator

Charles Wadsworth, beloved chamber music impresario, to retire

For 50 years, he's been doing this: the collegial rehearsals, the sound checks under museum rotundas, the ritual travel and lunches and visits with friends, the nonchalant but purposeful banter and joking designed to make the music accessible.

It began in 1960 when Gian Carlo Menotti asked a young Charles Wadsworth to organize a chamber music series for the Festival of Two Worlds in Spoleto, Italy. It continued when Wadsworth founded the Chamber Music Society of Lincoln Center in 1969 and reached new heights when he joined Spoleto Festival USA in 1977 as artistic director for chamber music.

And for years now, Wadsworth, a formidable pianist, has taken his show on the road, to Old Lyme, Conn., Savannah, Beaufort, Camden and Columbia.

Four years ago, he was lured by a friend to Cartagena, Colombia, a colonial city established in the 1500s that has become an economic and cultural center of the Caribbean. Wadsworth was charmed by the place and agreed to start a music festival there, his fourth, performing with his usual company in the Teatro Heredia, three old chapels and the historic Plaza San Pedro Claver, inside the walled city.

In May, Wadsworth turns 80. The cartilage in his knees has disappeared. Stairs and long walks are no longer an option. The demands of regular tours are starting to get to him. So this year's Spoleto Festival USA will be his last. This year, the beloved patriarch of chamber music, mentor to hundreds, will relinquish — reluctantly, with mixed feelings, with "deserved blues" — his public role as raconteur and master of ceremonies.

After 50 years of chamber music advocacy, after relaying to his loyal audiences countless anecdotes, jokes, insights and historical tidbits, after opening a vast repertoire of musical gems and inviting us to admire the glitter, explaining to us the reasons for such colors and brilliance, Wadsworth is trusting that we know enough now to keep on listening, unintimidated, eager to discover the intimate and inventive ideas of inspired minds.

No one else could have brought us to this point. The consensus among musicians is clear: Wadsworth has revolutionized classical music.

Aiming the spotlight

Let's put Wadsworth's accomplishment into perspective. The classical music you are likely most familiar with consists of the big works: Classical and Romantic symphonies, operas, concerti for violin or piano, perhaps some big choral works by Bach or Handel.

Yet the vast majority of the classical music repertoire is chamber music. For every symphony a composer has written, he has produced dozens of smaller works. Medieval, Renaissance and Baroque music is all meant for small and medium-size ensembles.

Before Wadsworth, most chamber music was relegated to conservatory recital halls and practice studios. What pieces made it to the big stage usually were scored for a string quartet or, sometimes, a piano trio, quartet or quintet. Even the vocal concert repertoire — those thousands of German *lieder*, French *melodie*, Italian *canzone*, English and American art songs — was heard infrequently by the wider public as singers devoted most of their energies to opera careers.

Wadsworth helped change that.

"I'm opposed to the idea that you have to have a certain sophistication to enjoy chamber music," he said.

He inspired musicians to delve deeply into a relatively untapped repertoire and enabled them to build specialized careers. And he revealed to listeners around the world, with humor and grace, that chamber music wasn't boring, esoteric or inaccessible, rather, it was perhaps the best way to gain an appreciation for the remarkably creative minds that found ways of expressing deep and exciting ideas through this intimate musical genre.

"Humor can relax people," he said.

Just ask pianist Wu Han. She and her husband, cellist David Finckel of Emerson String Quartet fame, are artistic directors of the Chamber

Music Society of Lincoln Center (where Wadsworth served as founding artistic director for 20 years).

She called Wadsworth's contributions "immeasurable." She said he possesses very good instincts about concert programming, musical talent and audience expectations. She described him as "funny, friendly and lovable" and universally known in music circles. She attributed the flexibility among musicians and their musical development today in part to his mentorship and vision.

Many musicians "could not have become what they are today without Charles," Han said.

Wadsworth made chamber music cool. He showed musicians that they could flourish as performers not only playing the solo repertoire, but by collaborating with colleagues.

A great collaborator himself, Wadsworth performs regularly. At the Columbia Museum of Art earlier this month, he played Francis Poulenc's Sonata for Clarinet and Piano with Todd Palmer. Wads-worth has a special affinity for French music. Poulenc, Maurice Ravel and Gabriel Faure appear often on his programs. Though he is from Newnan, Ga., he caresses the keyboard like a Frenchman, eliciting a supple and fluid sound, reveling in the modal harmonies.

Han said he plays with a natural sound and style. The two pianists played Claude Debussy's "Petite Suite" for four hands about six years ago.

"Charles has the most glorious sound and charming sense of timing, just like him — all warm and fuzzy," she said. Playing with Wadsworth always is fun and musically rewarding, Han added. But, she said, the experience is more than that: It's full of love.

When Alice Tully Hall in New York, built with Wadsworth's Chamber Music Society in mind, reopened after extensive renovations earlier this year, the patriarch was on stage for the Feb. 24 "Coming Home" concert presented by the society. He played the same piece he presented 40 years earlier when he first mounted the stage there: Bach's Trio Sonata in C major for Flute, Violin and Continuo, BWV 1037.

The program also included recently commissioned works by contemporary composers William Bolcom and George Tsontakis. Diverse programming is a Wadsworth hallmark that Han and her husband have continued to promote. And the contemporary works also have their roots with Wadsworth, for he initiated a commissioning program early on to ensure that living composers wrote chamber pieces.

Among the composers who have written for Wadsworth are Bolcom, Darius Mihaud, Pierre Boulez, Leonard Bernstein, Samuel Barber, John Corigliano, Luciano Berio, Lukas Foss, George Crumb and Chick Corea. In all, he commissioned about 150 works during his tenure with the society, Han said.

His professional success can be attributed to the usual suspects: hard work, luck, good timing, helpful colleagues and an appreciative audience. He would reach a pinnacle of the classical music work quickly and stay there. But there would be struggles along the way, especially in his private life.

Early years

Charles Wadsworth was born in Barnsville, Ga. His father, Charles Spurgeon Eugene William Wadsworth, was a clerk, a "fruit-and-vegetable man," at the U-Save-It Grocery. The family moved to Newnan when Charles was still very young. About 60 years later, the town would rename its renovated art-deco auditorium after its prodigal son, who returns regularly for concerts there.

His mother, Ethel Capps Wadsworth, worked in a ladies clothing store but aspired to a more specialized set of skills. So she attended a two-week training course in Atlanta at the Gossett Corset Co. and became a corsettiere. Charles received an early sex education, he said.

"At 6 or 7, I would sit in a corner of the fitting room when mother was lacing women into their corsets," he said.

His mother sang in church. His father played a little country fiddle, but wasn't very serious about it. One day, he absentmindedly laid the violin on a steamer trunk. When the top came down, "that stopped daddy's career cold," Wadsworth said.

But the son showed talent. In high school, he liked to accompany singers. Eventually, he would attend the Juilliard School in New York. To earn money, he worked gigs with singers at the Rotary Club and Lion's Club.

In 1954, he played at Riverside Church, where Richard Weagly led the choir. Weagly, a tenor, was organizing a recital at Town Hall and asked

Wadsworth to accompany him. Virgil Thompson, then-music critic for *The New York Times*, happened to attend the recital. In his review, Thompson wrote that Wadsworth's dynamic playing complemented Weag-ly's modest tenor perfectly. Thus began "a great period of recitals," Wadsworth said. "After the review, the phone was ringing off the wall."

A Juilliard recital with the great soprano Shirley Verrett led to years of touring with her. He played with Richard Tucker and Teresa Stratas, with Jan Pierce, Montserrat Caballe and Beverly Sills. Later, he would accompany other singers: Dietrich Fischer-Dieskau, Herman Prey, Shirley Verrett, Frederica von Stade, Kathleen Battle and Jessye Norman.

One day as Wadsworth played an upright piano in the pit of a Broadway theater, accompanying a singer auditioning for the Festival of Two Worlds, Gian Carlo Menotti took notice. Menotti didn't much care about the singer; he was interested in the young pianist who sounded so good.

"Young man, would you mind giving me your name and telephone number?" Menotti said. When he called, he told Wadsworth that he had never heard that aria played so beautifully. Menotti asked the pianist if he would be interested in preparing a group of singers for a production of his opera, "The Last Savage," which was scheduled to open at the Metropolitan Opera. Though the opera was no critical success, Menotti was delighted with Wadsworth and in 1959 invited him to Italy, where the accompanist would work with dancers and singers.

Shortly after the festival ended that year, Menotti called Wadsworth again, this time with an ambitious proposal to create a chamber music series of daily concerts.

One thing led to another. When William Shuman, head of Lincoln Center, heard about the success of the chamber series in Italy, Wadsworth received another phone call and another invitation. A new hall was being built, funded by Alice Tully. Its primary purpose was to offer a venue for chamber music.

His mother knew about her son's appointment as artistic director of the Chamber Music Society, but died before she could see him in action.

Wadsworth drew a lesson for young pianists from his early years: "Be sure when auditioning to give it everything you have."

A new world

Great success is always the result of hard work, but it usually takes some luck, too.

In Italy, Charles Wadsworth's success as a chamber music impresario was almost accidental. Festival of Two Worlds founder Gian Carlo Menotti had insisted that the concerts in Spoleto, Italy, have no printed programs. He wanted them to be informal, and he wanted Wadsworth to make audiences comfortable.

But there was a problem.

"I didn't speak Italian," Wadsworth said. "I made horrible gaffs."

The concerts — and his gaffs — were broadcast throughout Italy on the radio in those days. During one performance, he was describing a piece that called for a portable organ, among other instruments. Perhaps he didn't know the right Italian word, or forgot that it's nearly identical to the English equivalent. He had meant to say "organo" but cited instead an example of an organ: He said "ventro" — uterus — and the audience laughed.

"I developed a reputation as a great comedian," he said. And, *voila!*, chamber music wasn't anymore an austere and inaccessible genre. What's more, Wadsworth's diverse programming, which featured a variety of instrument combinations, was new to patrons, some of whom might have been familiar with a few string quartets or piano trios but had little exposure in this context to clarinets, harps, odd percussion instruments and portable organs.

"By the end of the second year, the concerts were always sold out," he said.

Meanwhile, in New York City, Susan Popkin was gaining a reputation as another innovative promoter of the arts. Popkin grew up listening to classical music and playing piano. She attended Mannes College, The New School of Music, where she met a plethora of talented artists struggling to launch careers.

In 1961, she decided to forgo her own performance career to help others. She started the Young Concert Artists, providing the bridge for the most talented singers and instrumentalists to cross into the professional world of music. Initially, she worked with a $5,000 budget but grew the nonprofit organization over the years. Today, it remains one of the world's foremost promoters of young musicians who must pass a rigorous audition process to become eligible for representation.

In 1963, Popkin found herself in Spoleto, Italy, helping out during rehearsals and concerts, turning pages for musicians. When Wadsworth, the members of a string quartet and a singer gathered to rehearse the "Chanson Perpetuelle" by Ernest Chausson, Popkin's acute musical ear perked up. The pianist had a consummate sense of timing; he was expressive but never domineering, and he demonstrated a thorough grasp of the chamber music repertoire.

"I was very impressed with the way Charles sounded," she said.

Wadsworth perked up, too.

"She was obviously brilliant, funny and just happened to be very beautiful," he said.

They married in 1966, three years before the Chamber Music Society of Lincoln Center offered its first performance. Susan Wadsworth would turn pages at almost every Chamber Music Society concert for the first 10 of her husband's 20 years with the organization. And Charles would attend all semifinal and final round auditions held by Young Concert Artists, identifying and recruiting dozens of talented chamber music artists over many years.

In 1971, they had a daughter, Rebecca, who would grow up in elite company, travel the world, marry, divorce, raise a son and eventually work with her mother in the offices of Young Concert Artists.

Rebecca vividly remembers a day she looked out from the family's apartment above Piazza del Duomo in Spoleto, Italy, to see the sunlight slanting across the cobblestones and striking the Romanesque facade of the cathedral. Starlings swooped in the air above, their arrowlike bodies decorating the darkening sky in playful unison.

Never easy

His marriage to Susan was his second.

Wadsworth met his first wife, Sarah, when they were students at the University of Georgia in Athens. A fine pianist herself, Sarah attended Juilliard, too, but decided to forgo a music career to take care of her family.

The couple had two children, David, born in 1955, and Beryl, born in 1964. As a newborn, David showed signs of developmental problems. Before long, he was diagnosed as "moderately to severely retarded" and unlikely to be able to care for himself in life.

It was Wadsworth's saddest moment, and it led to discord and difficulty at home. The boy could not connect emotionally, and "at a certain point it became obvious that he had to live away," Wadsworth said.

David was sent to a special school in Pennsylvania, part of the Waldorf education system based on the philosophy of Austrian Rudolph Steiner. Camphill Village was an "idyllic place," Wadsworth said. When David was older, he transferred to another Camphill facility near Copake, N.Y., where he continues to do well, according to his father. Wadsworth has long supported the facility, organizing high-profile fundraisers that feature some of his musical colleagues.

The difficulty Charles and Sarah faced with their son was too much for the marriage. After 13 years together, the couple split up, shortly after Beryl was born. Sarah moved with her daughter to Dallas.

Now nearly 80, Wadsworth has been designated by France as a Chevalier in the Order of Arts and Letters and by Italy as a Cavaliere Ufficiale in the Order of Merit. He has received the Handel Medallion from New York City and South Carolina's Order of the Palmetto and Elizabeth O'Neill Verner Award. He has three honorary doctorates. He was been invited to perform at the White House for Presidents Kennedy, Nixon, Ford, Carter and Reagan.

For that last White House performance, he brought along Beryl. She was 16 or 17 at the time, and the concert was a mesmerizing highlight of her early years, she said. Beryl had seen her father just six or seven times during her first 18 years, and always for short visits. During Beryl's childhood, her mother kept her away from Wadsworth, she said.

"As a child, all I knew was that he was very, very famous — and not around," she said.

Many years later, after spiritual detours and schooling disruptions, after visits with her father that finally helped start a relationship, after her mother's fatal battle with breast cancer and soon before the birth of her two children, Beryl found herself in one of Carnegie Hall's velvet seats watching her brother take a bow. It was a benefit concert in support of Camphill Village, and performers had invited village residents on stage to play handheld instruments such as bells and small harps. The sight of it touched Beryl deeply.

Protégés

The formula Wadsworth discovered in Italy — casual humor, informative conversation — proved its worth tenfold in the U.S., first at Lincoln Center, then at the Spoleto Festival.

Wadsworth has nurtured a loyal, large and admiring population of patrons eager to hear the witty jokes, witness his unassuming manner and listen to well-performed music. The recipe might have been too sweet for some, but it was easy to swallow. What's more, it helped the players. Musicians perform better when they relax and forge true connections with their audiences, he said. The key is simple communication.

Edward Arron, a talented cellist who will take the reins of the Charles Wadsworth and Friends series, said chamber music is all about communication. The players must be well-attuned to one another, and their instruments, each with its own voice, in dialogue. They must convey the composer's intentions and their own emotions and interpretation, to audiences who, in turn, react to what they hear, fueling the performance.

Arron said that his mentor has developed a sure-fire formula.

"He has put chamber music in a context that audiences love and presents it unpretentiously," Arron said. "I think he's made chamber music lovers out of thousands and thousands of people."

Nigel Redden, director of Spoleto Festival USA and the Lincoln Center Festival, said Wadsworth was the "pater familia" of chamber music who has succeeded in demystifying the concert experience, removing any threat.

"There is kind of a family quality to the whole enterprise," Redden said.

The prevailing rumor is that violinist Geoff Nuttall of the St. Lawrence String Quartet, intimately familiar as a player with the festival and well-practiced in public banter, will take over for Wadsworth as Charleston's chamber music impresario.

The last concert of Wadsworth's last Spoleto Festival will end the way the first one began: with the masterful, two-cello String Quintet in C major by Franz Schubert, the last work the composer wrote before his death at 31 in 1828.

Emotion and fantasy

About 350 turned out for a March 12 concert at the Columbia Museum of Art. Skip Beach, who has worked with Wadsworth for 12 years, recorded the performance for future radio broadcast.

Wadsworth introduced the musicians: Of pianist Gilles Vonsattel, he said, "You will hear a very strange accent; he was born in Switzerland." He called Edward Arron his "associate legend." He explained that he was there when violinist Karen Gomyo made her professional breakthrough at 14, and how clarinetist Todd Palmer has been part of the Wadsworth team since the early 1990s. When the clapping died down, Wadsworth said, "I'm not sure the applause was necessary: It might go to his head."

Then he described the traditionally classical first movement of Beethoven's Trio in B Flat Major, op. 11. "Nothing particularly interesting is happening," he said with a wink. "I don't mean that."

Just before intermission, Wadsworth said, "We'll come back and have some more fun, unless you're miserable so far."

The next day in Columbia, Wadsworth said he was enduring moments of disturbing sadness. The frenetic travel to Connecticut, Georgia and South Carolina would end soon. Programming concerts, coordinating musicians, researching composers' lives and works — all of it would be delegated to others, left in their capable hands, no longer his concern.

"The last weekend in Charleston is going to be full of incredibly deep emotions as I hang it up there," he said.

Daughter Beryl said he planned on using his retirement as an opportunity to spend more time with his family, especially his grandchildren, Aria, 9, and Aliya, 7.

Wadsworth fantasizes about being a bartender in Palm Beach, Fla., playing piano in the lounge and becoming a masseur.

"If I really did massage, I'd want to choose my own customers." People would have to apply in person, or send a resume with photos, he said, chuckling.

But it is obvious that for Wadsworth, music is the fire that keeps him warm and full of life.

Of course, he will continue to play and attend the auditions held by Young Concert Artists, and give lectures when invited and perhaps encourage a few more audiences to enjoy the music.

The Johnson Collection

How South Carolina's largest private art collection transformed an old mill town

SPARTANBURG — Nestled in the rolling terrain beneath the Blue Ridge Mountains, this South Carolina town once was known for its 40 textile mills and industrious residents who, in the years after the Civil War, served King Cotton with enough devotion to transform an Upstate urban relic of the Revolutionary War into a prosperous and influential hub of commerce.

But by the 1950s, textile manufacturing in Spartanburg was becoming difficult to justify. Local wages and operating costs were rising; overseas, though, manufacturing costs were low. So Spartanburg's industrial activity diminished and, ultimately, disappeared. The mills became ruins that generated only memories, and then not even that.

For three decades Spartanburg could boast little but its nickname, Hub City, a remnant of its textile days when rail lines crisscrossed through the town. But today, the city is known for something else, something unexpected, something that has nothing to do with its origins or industry. Located here is the state's largest private collection of fine art, and a lot of it is on view around town.

In the 1980s, George Dean Johnson Jr. and his wife Susan (Susu) Phifer Johnson decided to make their hometown a base of operations.

The real estate company, Johnson Development Associates, started to build industrial structures, office buildings, multifamily communities and self-storage facilities. The company insisted on investing in Spartanburg. It acquired property in and around town on which retail centers were built. It secured land for BMW's North American manufacturing plant. It constructed housing to ensure that people who worked in Spartanburg could live in Spartanburg.

Other Johnson ventures, including OTO Development, American Credit Acceptance and WJ Partners, also flourished, watering the family's deepening roots in the city.

All the while, Susu Johnson collected art, lots of art, building a magnificent private collection of works, mostly paintings, associated with the American South. The Johnsons' daughter, Susanna, who studied art history, fundraising and philanthropy at college, encouraged her parents to make their artwork available to the public.

In 2002, The Johnson Collection became a limited liability company. The collection now consists of 1,200 pieces dating back to the late 1700s. It includes a huge variety of styles, time periods and cultural and regional references.

But don't think all this art is sequestered away in a private residence somewhere for the sole enjoyment of the Johnson family. What began as a simple interest in collecting fine art of the Carolinas has become a public enterprise. The inventory has grown so much that it requires a small staff to manage it.

The enterprise is unusual. It's not a nonprofit. It has no board of directors. It can't accept donations. It provides no tax benefit to its operators. It generates no revenue. Rather, it is a philanthropic venture with millions of dollars in annual expenditures.

The Johnson Collection organizes exhibitions, publishes catalogs, lends work to other institutions and flings open its doors to scholars. It also hangs paintings at a variety of nearby venues, including Converse and Wofford colleges, the George Dean Johnson Jr. College of Business and Economics at the University of South Carolina Upstate, the new AC Hotel in downtown Spartanburg, a small charter school in the area and other locations.

The Johnson Development Associates' four-story office building in the heart of the city, One Morgan Square, is a central repository of art in the collection. Pictures hang in the lobby and in the corridors and in the private offices. The small suite occupied by The Johnson Collection staff includes a climate-controlled storage room with sliding partitions. A small gallery steps away on Main Street displays a fraction of the works, often in partnership with a community organization.

"They truly see themselves as stewards, not owners," said Lynne Blackman, the collection's spokesperson.

Today, Spartanburg, which also is home to Denny's corporate headquarters, an impressive cultural center and a regionally famous independent book shop and publisher, is really Arts Hub City.

The city sponsors public art projects to enliven the refurbished downtown area and welcomes opportunities to engage residents through the arts.

In 2016 and 2017, the Chapman Cultural Center spearheaded "See Spartanburg in a New Light," a project that featured nine outdoor installations by artist Erwin Redl, the result of a $1 million Bloomberg Philanthropies grant.

But nothing in Spartanburg, or anywhere else in South Carolina, compares to The Johnson Collection.

In May 2016, they doubled down on their commitment to make the collection publicly accessible by gifting the enormous "Battle of Gettysburg" painting by James Walker to the Spartanburg County Public Libraries. The 20-foot-long painting, carefully restored after The Johnson Collection acquired it in 2004, is displayed in a custom-made room that includes two interactive touchscreen kiosks that provide a host of information about the sprawling battle scene. To say it's an educational tool is an understatement.

In December 2017, the $20 million, 10-story AC Hotel opened, featuring a traditional brick exterior and a slick, modernist interior. The lobby and bar areas on the main floor and common space on the mezzanine feature more than 40 works of art from The Johnson Collection, all of which were produced between 1933 and 1957 by the artists at Black Mountain College in North Carolina. The school was an unconventional, non-hierarchical, boundary-pushing enclave that attracted faculty and students who would prove very influential, such as Josef and Anni Albers, Robert Motherwell, Cy Twombly, Ruth Asawa, Willem and Elaine de Kooning, Robert Rauschenberg, Jacob Lawrence, Walter Gropius, Merce Cunningham, John Cage and Buckminster Fuller.

Attracting attention

The Johnson Collection is so substantial and of such high quality that serious museum curators and scholars of American art know all about it. One is Sylvia Yount, curator of the Metropolitan Museum of Art's American Wing.

"I so admire what TJC has done in the past few years, prioritizing scholarship and strategic collecting as they've matured from a little-known private collection to one that's become more active in the broader American art field through loans, exhibitions, and publications that recover long overlooked Southern production," Yount wrote in an email.

She has studied, and borrowed, the 19th-century painting by William D. Washington called "The Burial of Latane," which Yount called an icon of Civil War imagery, as well as Henry Mosler's stunning "The Lost Cause."

In 2017, she delivered the lecture titled "A Region of Their Own: Southern Women Artists 1890-1940" at The Johnson Collection's annual Voices in American Art symposium, and then contributed the foreword to the catalog "Central to Their Lives," which accompanies a current touring show.

That exhibit, at the Georgia Museum of Art in Athens until Sept. 23, will travel to the Mississippi Museum of Art in Jackson, the Huntington Museum of Art in West Virginia, the Dixon Gallery and Gardens in Memphis, Tenn., and then the Gibbes Museum of Art in Charleston, where it will be on view in early 2020. It makes two more stops after that, in Jacksonville, Fla., and in Roanoke, Va.

"I think it's fair to say that most of the women represented by work in the current TJC exhibition have received little attention outside of regional museums in the South, if there, despite their often national reputations in their own day," Yount wrote in her email. "The exhibition and, most importantly, accompanying publication (the permanent record of the project) ... should do a great deal to ensure that more academics, curators, collectors and general art lovers are better aware of their lives and work."

Angela Mack, director of the Gibbes Museum and a Spartanburg native, said the Johnsons are among the art collectors who really know what they're doing. They don't acquire works willy-nilly; there is method to the madness.

Peggy Guggenheim, Leonard Lauter, Samuel Henry Kress — they all had a particular focus, acquiring "a concentrated group of objects," which gave their collections depth and substance, she said. The Johnsons have done the same with their emphasis on Southern art.

"That really is the mark of a good collector: somebody who really learns a particular area well," Mack said.

The Gibbes Museum has worked with The Johnson Collection on several occasions, sometimes consulting informally with one another, sometimes collaborating formally, Mack said. The museum has hosted two previous exhibitions of work from the collection during the last decade or so. "Central to Their Lives" will be the third.

"It's going to be a real testament to what women have done in the South for a very long time," Mack said of the show. "And I think people are going to be surprised when they see it all together."

Geordy Johnson, CEO of Johnson Development Associates, said the show is an important reflection of his mother's feminist concerns.

"It's a life priority for my mother, promoting women's interests," he said.

Wanting to share

Leo Twiggs, an Orangeburg-based artist known for his batik paintings that often present themes relevant to the South, is among a number of African-American artists whose work can be found in The Johnson Collection.

Two years ago, he completed a nine-painting series called "Requiem for Mother Emanuel" which was a reflection on the 2015 murders of nine members of Emanuel AME Church in Charleston. By the time the series was exhibited at the City Gallery at Waterfront Park, all but three of the works had been sold.

That's when Lynne Blackman swooped into action, arranging for the purchase of the remaining three paintings. But she didn't stop there.

Concerned that only one public viewing of the powerful series had been arranged, Blackman went to Susu Johnson to pitch an idea.

Before long, the complete series was on display at the TJC Gallery on Main Street and then sent to The Mint Museum in Charlotte. The response in both places was tremendous, Twiggs and Blackman said.

It helped that the Carolina Panthers head coach Ron Rivera and several players went to see the paintings in Spartanburg, and that a video of their visit was broadcast by ESPN.

"The Johnson Collection was instrumental in taking Mother Emanuel and putting it in the national eye," Twiggs said. And it kept the series together for nearly two years, he added. "Lynne was tenacious about getting it out so the public could see it. ... She felt it should have a wider audience."

Neither Wofford College nor Converse College have a scholar of American art on their faculties, so The Johnson Collection has created a part-time curatorial position (currently vacant) for an Americanist who can teach courses at the nearby schools, according to Chief Operating Officer Sarah Tignor.

"We're cultivating an interest among students in Southern art," she said.

The downtown gallery is used for the same purpose, luring not just students but many others to the small space where they can admire a range of paintings regardless of their level of expertise. Currently, the gallery is collaborating with The Children's Museum of the Upstate on a special show that features key abstract works from the collection and a variety of paintings by young people modeled on the masterpieces.

In this way, and in many other ways, The Johnson Collection demystifies great art, brings it to street level and encourages all to enjoy it.

"The thing about the Johnsons is that they want to share," Mack said. "They do it out of the goodness of their hearts, and that is just tremendous."

Making Sense of It

After Charleston church shooting, artists help
public digest the horror

Sometimes an event is so profound, so remarkable, it captures the imagination of many, including those who were not impacted directly.

Sometimes such an event is so traumatic that it ruptures the collective psyche and causes a whole nation to wonder about itself.

The Triangle Shirtwaist Factory Fire of 1911 did this. The 1963 bombing of 16th Street Baptist Church in Birmingham, which left four little girls dead, did this. Columbine did this, and then Sandy Hook, then the Pulse nightclub, and later Parkland. 9/11 did this.

And the Emanuel AME Church shootings did this, too.

"Some events are so egregious, so in opposition to social morality, that they became symbols of the need for social change," said Von Bakanic, a sociology professor at the College of Charleston. And it's often the artists who first offer "a set of ideas about why this is wrong and what happens if we don't stop it." When the tension between a dangerous ideology and the values of a just society becomes intolerable, artists take charge, Bakanic said. "They set up the direction of a new ideology."

That tension has caused many social eruptions. Women garment workers locked inside a dangerous building with no way out except through the windows to their death shocked the nation. Four young lives destroyed by those who viewed African Americans as the enemy shocked the nation. Young men with minds so twisted they chose to fire semi-automatic weapons at students in school shocked the nation. Terrorists who perverted Islam and believed that mass murder would bring them a heavenly reward shocked the nation.

How could someone welcomed into a Bible study class shoot nine people dead, just like that?

After the fact, we can learn much, we can investigate, gather information, piece together a motive, contextualize the violence. But still, we are left with an essential enigma, an unanswerable question.

And so the artists get to work, for this enigma is part of their domain. The artists write songs and poems and books, they make paintings and sculptures, they peer into the soul of America and depict what they see, they raise more questions, they challenge the rest of us to think deeper, they rant and rave, laugh and cry, and sometimes cause us to do the same.

This is how Emanuel has found its way into popular culture. Four years later, the shooting remains — and will always remain — one of those watershed moments we will forever ponder.

Timing is everything, Bakanic said.

"You have to consider the socio-cultural history at the time of the event," she said. "Emanuel came at a particular moment in history: Obama was president, and there was a tremendous surge in hate groups in response to that."

And the number of hate groups has been increasing ever since.

"With Emanuel, the murders were so egregious — they happened after this person spent over an hour in Bible study with his victims, and he still murdered his victims, and he did it to try to start a race war." The shooting came at a moment when many in the country were debating whether we were part of a "post-racial society," Bakanic observed. Yet large racial issues remained unresolved, and this galvanized the nation's attention and grief, prompting Americans to ponder their condition, and motivating artists to take action.

President Barack Obama pondered the status of the nation when he delivered the eulogy at the Rev. Clementa Pinckney's funeral and sang a famous hymn. Childish Gambino seems to have pondered it when he made the video for his hit song "This is America." In it, he fires a machine gun blast at a church choir, an oblique reference to Emanuel, many have said. Joan Baez pondered this moment when she decided to record Zoe Mulford's song "The President Sang Amazing Grace."

Leo Twiggs, a batik artist in Orangeburg, couldn't escape it. Here was yet another example of African Americans targeted by an extremist, another set of victims, another consequence of the nation's failure to reconcile its history with its declared values. Twiggs got to work making a series of nine paintings, partly to work through his distress, partly to depict the power of community, the ways in which the sins of the past can be turned into a cross of redemption — if only we would make the effort.

Rhiannon Giddens was thinking about the shooting when, in exasperation, she recorded "Cry No More" in the sanctuary of United Congregational Church in her hometown of Greensboro, N.C., with help from a choir and a drum. The song recounts all that black people in America have endured over the centuries: First they stole our bodies, then they stole our sons, then they stole our gods and gave us new ones, then they stole our beauty, the comfort in our skin, and then they gave us duty, and then they gave us sin. And now, Giddens is telling us, add Emanuel to the list.

"The massacre at the AME church in Charleston is just the latest in a string of racially charged events that have broken my heart," she said shortly after the shooting. "There are a lot of things to fix in this world, but history says if we don't address this canker, centuries in the making, these things will continue to happen. No matter what level privilege you have, when the system is broken everybody loses. We all have to speak up when injustice happens. No matter what. And music is one of the best ways I know to do so."

Artist Carrie Mae Weems responded to the shooting by creating a theater piece called "Grace Notes" that premiered at Spoleto Festival in 2016. South Carolina Poet Laureate Marjorie Wentworth was driven to her pen immediately after hearing about the crime at Emanuel. She wrote "Holy City," dedicated to the victims and first published by The Post and Courier. Charleston Poet Laureate Marcus Amaker also wrote a poem, "Black Cloth," about racism and intolerance, but also faith and love. So did Nikky Finney, for the Halsey Institute of Contemporary Art's "Southbound" show; it's titled "Miss Polly is Akimbo Underneath the Mother Emanuel Collection Table." Local rock band Dead 27s wrote a commemorative song, "Emanuel." Gospel singer Shirley Caesar responded to the event with "Mother Emanuel."

And then there are the books. Wentworth joined Herb Frazier and Bernard Powers to produce "We Are Charleston: Tragedy and Triumph at Mother Emanuel." Post and Courier reporter Jennifer Berry Hawes wrote "Grace Will Lead Us Home: The Charleston Church Massacre and the Hard, Inspiring Journey to Forgiveness." And now there is a documentary film, "Emanuel," directed by Brian Ivie.

It is a safe bet that much more will follow.

"It shows you a level of impact the event still has," said the Rev. Kylon Middleton, pastor of Mt. Zion AME Church and a close friend of Emanuel's pastor, The Rev. Clementa Pinckney, who was among the nine killed. "With some things, the farther you move away from them, the more they fade, but other events last. This remains something that's fascinating, to the extent that people are trying to find a way to understand how these people can move from a very traumatic moment to lives that are filled with a pursuit for justice, activism that is productive and not destructive, and a hope that somehow the very system that created this evil person can also restore (our faith in it)."

Middleton said these manifestations of the tragedy in popular culture serve an important purpose.

"Every time we think we forget, someone reminds us," he said. "They remind us in a song, they remind us in a painting." And they force us to confront the horror of it, Middleton added. "At some point we have to get to the root of the evil, which is hate, and hate steeped in bigotry."

Maybe that is the artist's implicit plea: to get to the root of it. Twiggs would have us do this. He has been getting to the root of it in his art for decades. His "Crossings" series, and "Targeted Man" series, and "Commemoration" series all address the perversions of history and the racism embedded in American culture. "Requiem for Mother Emanuel," then, was but a continuation of his work.

"Mother Emanuel is not just a singular incident," he said. "South Carolina is the place where the Civil War began. It was first state to secede from the Union. It has had a raucous past." What's more, the Legislature rarely has passed laws that explicitly benefit black people unless they were forced to do so, Twiggs said. Consider the Confederate Flag debate. Look at the state of public education.

But poor-quality schools don't often inspire songs and paintings.

Emanuel is something else, Twiggs said, something hideous on its face, but also symbolic of generations of cruelty.

"It resonates because of this long history, because it happened in Charleston, because it killed people in a prayer service setting, and because the pastor of the church was a member of the Legislature, and a well-liked and well-respected member of the Legislature, I might add," he said. "This is one of the things folklore is made of."

Lost Homes

Charleston artist recalls destructive impact of roadway projects

A ndrea Hazel was a teenager when the highway was built. The road project required a wide clearance down the neck of the Charleston peninsula and then across to the Ashley River.

The problem was that this was a residential area full of houses. At least 150 of them would be demolished to make way for Interstate 26 and the Crosstown, constructed during the middle 1960s.

Hazel watched it happen from her home on Ashley Avenue.

She watched as the plans were laid and the bulldozers did their work. She watched as families were forced to seek refuge elsewhere.

She watched as old Charleston neighborhoods — Elliottborough, North-Central and the Westside, each full of single-family homes and small businesses — were ruptured by the roadway.

"Our church used to be on Sheppard Street," she recalled. "Now it's the Crosstown."

The infrastructure project was completed by the end of 1968. This was the era of school desegregation, and white residents on the upper part of Charleston's peninsula already were moving to the suburbs. The Crosstown project accelerated White Flight, depressing property values and exacerbating the city's racial divide.

A few years ago, Hazel came across a trove of photographs kept in the Margaretta Childs Archives at the Historic Charleston Foundation. These were images of the soon-to-be demolished houses, many featuring the surveyors who assessed the properties and determined their fate. A few included homeowners: women drying clothes on the line, children playing in the yard, men wondering at the purpose of the clipboards and measuring tape.

Hazel was captivated by the pictures of her old stomping grounds, and decided to put her brush to work. She painted one watercolor, then another, then another.

"The idea was not to point a finger and blame, but to show what happened, and to remember these places," she said.

She has made eight paintings so far in her series "How It Was: Charleston in 1963," and hopes to reach at least 20.

Bulldozer's banner year

"It's really a great thing she's doing," said Karen Emmons, archivist and librarian at the Historic Charleston Foundation. "To me, they bring the photos to life, so I get a sense of human beings living in those houses."

Emmons said the entire archive contains nearly 2,300 images, of which 602 are of properties affected by the I-26 and Crosstown construction. All of the photographs can be accessed via the Lowcountry Digital Library

It was tricky cataloging them all, she said. The photos, which were donated to the foundation by the South Carolina Department of Transportation, contained little identifying information. So the foundation partnered with Kevin Eberle, a professor at the Charleston School of Law and an obsessive amateur historian who has spent much of his free time chronicling the upper part of the Charleston peninsula, where he lives.

He wrote a book, published by The History Press in 2012, called "The History of Hampton Park." And he gives walking and bicycling tours of the upper peninsula.

For the old DOT photographs to be useful to historians and others, the properties they capture for posterity needed to be explicitly identified, so Eberle cross-referenced them with historical maps, especially Sanborn maps, created by the Sanborn Fire Insurance Company to assess liability in urban areas.

The maps included enough clues, such as exact building footprint, adjacent fire hydrants, materials used, ingress and egress, to help Eberle locate nearly all of the properties in the DOT pictures.

For whatever reason, perhaps a half-dozen of the photographed buildings, "cheek-by-jowl up against the road," managed to avoid demolition, he said. "But otherwise all of the buildings that they photographed ended up getting the bulldozer treatment."

The conventional wisdom is that the affected area was predominantly black and the properties mostly dilapidated. This notion helped planners justify the infrastructure project, which would connect I-26 to Highway 17, in terms of urban renewal and improvement.

But Eberle is not sure there was any malicious intent. This was a middle- and working-class neighborhood that included white residents. Some of the housing stock was quite nice, some of it in disrepair. Some homes were modernized, others had no central plumbing.

"If you go through the photos, (you see that) the housing stock really is indistinguishable from the housing stock remaining today," Eberle said. "It was not one squalid tenement house after another."

What is certain is that African Americans were disproportionately impacted by the new roadway. Property compensation went to owners, not renters, and that left many blacks out in the cold, Eberle noted. They were less able than their white counterparts to afford a new single-family home in West Ashley or elsewhere, at a time when the size of the city was much smaller and housing options fewer. And those who remained in the neighborhood took a financial hit.

"Having a road in the middle of your neighborhood certainly is not going to drive up property values," Eberle said.

Arguably, none of the affected properties had much historical value individually, he said. Collectively, though, the once-cohesive neighborhood was an essential part of the city's character and identity. "The collective scope of the demolition ranks up there with (the loss of) the Charleston Orphanage and other examples (of) terrible, what-were-they-thinking demolition stories. The bulldozer industry must have had a banner year that year, because they were going whole hog knocking things down."

Winslow Hastie, president and CEO of Historic Charleston Foundation, said Eberle's efforts were essential and appreciated.

"It's a sad fact, but the not-as-wealthy neighborhoods, particularly African American neighborhoods, were not as well documented at the time," Hastie said. "Recognizing the damage that was wrought by these infrastructure projects is important."

He said the effort to create a new greenway, called the Lowcountry

LowLine, along a portion of the I-26 right of way is meant, in part, to acknowledge the damage that was done and reconnect the streets cleaved in two by construction of the highway.

Hastie, a member of the LowLine's board, said he and his colleagues want to "document the story and use the project as a way to stitch back together the neighborhood."

'What the devastation meant'

Walter Boags, a tour guide, bartender and cousin of Andrea Hazel, said he lived on Ashe Street between Coming and Rutledge avenues in 1963, when many of the DOT photographs were made. He attended A.B. Rhett Elementary School, then Burke. To get to his all-black school, he walked past the all-white Mitchell Elementary.

By the mid-1960s, some African-American families relocated from the peninsula to a black subdivision on James Island called Westchester.

"I knew the coming highway would be very big and impactful," he said. "I wasn't sophisticated enough at 11 to understand how, in some ways, it was aimed through the black community (for) urban renewal or slum removal. ... In a sense, the big highway coming through was kind of an adventure, in the way that bombed-out London was a playground for kids unable to fully appreciate what the devastation meant."

Hazel said the DOT photographs "speak to me." She knew instantly she needed to paint some of them.

"I like the questions that (the collection) puts up: Why is there a brick on that garbage can?" Why is that house overgrown? Who lived there? What were these residents thinking when they saw the surveyors in their yards, arms spread wide? "It creates a dialogue for me, and I hope other people see it too."

Hazel, the oldest of six children, attended college in New York, majored in math and became a school teacher. Along the way, she took an art appreciation class and visited her first museum, the Metropolitan Museum of Art. "I was just blown away," she recalled of the experience.

She graduated in 1970. Seven years later, she picked up a camera for the first time. She became a volunteer photographer for the nascent Piccolo Spoleto Festival. Eventually, people asked her to document private events, so she started a small photography business.

Hazel was busy, teaching at Trident Technical College and shooting weddings on the weekends, when, in 2001, a friend at church gave her a gift for her 53rd birthday: watercolor paint and brushes. The man, Frank Hamilton, was worried that Hazel was overtaxing herself, and that watercolor painting would relax her.

A few years later, they were married, and Hazel was a dedicated painter. She took classes at the College of Charleston to hone her technique. In 2005, she retired from teaching after 30 years. In 2008, she shut down her photo business.

She is fascinated by the intersection of art and community and determined to capture in watercolor the character and the history of the place she calls home.

"I want to remind people who we are," she said. "This Charleston is a very special place. I don't want to throw out everything we had."

Making Omar

The story behind Spoleto Festival's opera about an enslaved Muslim scholar in the Carolinas

She plucks a few notes on her banjo, humming.

The beginning of a melody emerges. Rhiannon Giddens sings words she has written about longing and sorrow and mystery and pain and faith.

A few more notes on the banjo, an instrument with African origins, and she is determining the rhythm and the shape of a phrase. Sometimes she doubles back and adds harmony.

The aria is taking form.

Here is Julie, a Christian now, singing about family, singing about her difficult life, offering advice to her new Muslim friend. Here is the sneering Charleston master, bitter, cruel. And here is Omar, trying to make sense of it all, trying to grasp who he was, who he is now.

Giddens plucks her banjo and, little by little, an opera is born.

* * *

When she is ready, Giddens opens the GarageBand app on her iPhone and touches "Record." At home in Ireland, she sings the melody, accompanying herself on banjo, committing these nascent compositions to a digital file she sends to her collaborator in California, Michael Abels, a composer of popular film scores.

Then she waits for a reply, nervous, not yet convinced.

Abels opens the file and listens to the recording with its clear voice, its lyricism. He responds, "This is great!" And she thinks, "OK, I'm not nuts."

Giddens, best-known as a practitioner of, and advocate for, African American folk music, finds time to write her first opera in between other obligations. Sometimes she is at home with the kids and her partner, the Italian musician Francesco Turrisi, when an idea comes to her;

sometimes she's on the road, in a hotel room somewhere, like Ithaca or Ann Arbor. Her schedule is full.

Little by little, the opera, which is based on the autobiography of Omar ibn Said, comes together. Giddens is writing the libretto, too, and it spills out in the form of a long poem, divided into chapters. She is a little uneasy. She wonders if she is afflicted with imposter's syndrome. But she is much more than a folk artist. She is not uncomfortable in this musical element. She has had her encounters with opera.

Still, this is the biggest thing she has ever done.

Omar was an educated and literate Muslim man who was snatched from his homeland in an arid region by the Senegal River in Africa. Arabic was not his first language, but he learned it mostly by memorizing the Quran and writing out its verses.

He grew up in a period of upheaval, but managed to further his education by traveling to various religious schools and embarking on a journey to understand the ways of Sufism, a mystical and peace-loving branch of Islam. He was 31 when he returned home. Five times a day he prayed, for six years. But the rituals would be interrupted in 1807, when infidels fell upon his village, slaughtered many, and enslaved the rest.

Now, five years after Spoleto Festival USA commissioned it — after research and consultations with experts on Islam, Western Africa and the slave trade, after auditions and workshops, writing and rewriting, digital transmissions between collaborators, deep dives into the historical record, a close reading of Omar's account of his life, and the interruptions of a global pandemic — "Omar" the opera is ready.

* * *

The project began because of an obsession, and it was realized because of the story it tells: how an educated African Muslim from the Futa Toro region located in the Senegal River basin was caught up in the transatlantic slave trade, landed at Charleston, escaped to North Carolina and eventually came to write an autobiographical essay.

The small book is a rare specimen. Few enslaved Africans could read or write, though Muslims were more likely to be literate. A small

214

fraction of those in bondage managed to create documents that survive today. None, except Omar ibn Said, wrote in Arabic. His essay was translated into English and acquired by the Library of Congress in 2017.

Omar likely came to Charleston in late 1807, just before the international slave trade ban took effect. He almost certainly arrived at Gadsden's Wharf, the sole Cooper River landing point for slave ships at the time. To beat the impending ban, so many ships sailed into the harbor with their human cargo that a massive quarantine facility was needed on the wharf and some slave auctions were held aboard the boats.

Omar's book sheds necessary light on something few people today know: The institution of American slavery shackled and imported more than 300,000 Africans, and perhaps a fifth of them were Muslims. As the population of enslaved people in the U.S. grew exponentially, Islam's influence spread like the roots of a tree in moist forest soil, even as the greening limbs received nourishment from Christianity.

After Zeyba Rahman, director of the Doris Duke Foundation's Building Bridges Program, introduces then-Spoleto Festival USA General Director Nigel Redden to Omar's work, Redden can't stop talking about it with whoever will listen to him.

When Giddens performs at the Gaillard Center during the 2017 festival, producer Nicole Taney and Redden greet her backstage and mention Omar.

An enslaved Muslim in America.

Giddens, a product of the American South, knows little about African Muslims forced across an ocean, turning toward the rising sun each morning to pray.

She is intrigued.

Soon after, Taney has an a-ha moment. The short autobiography could serve as the basis for an opera. And Giddens should write it. She is known for her thoughtful investigations into folk music traditions and for asserting the influences of African Americans. She is a storyteller, sharing tales of oppression and redemption through her songs. She is an excavator of history, a musical innovator, a classically trained vocalist.

"That is not a bad idea," Redden responds.

Taney lets the summer ripen before she reaches out to Giddens with an offer.

"I'm very interested!" Giddens emails back.

* * *

In April 2019, nearly a year before anyone could know of the approaching pandemic and its disruptions, Giddens attends a small workshop at Opera America on 7th Avenue in New York City at which the material is performed, discussed, adapted and reworked. Abels has arranged portions of the score for piano and strings, and this is the first time she hears her music come to life in the hands of others.

Tears come to her eyes, so many she must wipe them away again and again.

At the second workshop in New York City that September, Giddens, Abels, conductor John Kennedy and others involved in the production convene again at Opera America. Marc A. Scorca Hall is an intimate recital space with red and blue walls, a wood floor and a small stage where the musicians gather. A few dozen chairs are set up in rows, available for onlookers. Instrument cases are piled in a back corner.

They bring the simmering opera to a boil once more and corroborate its progress. They assess how each section flows into the next, how Omar's enslavement and journey from Africa to Charleston, and then to Fayetteville, N.C., reverberates in this small room. This time they work through the overture, the mother's aria, Omar's escape, the middle passage, the slave auction and Julie's aria.

Kennedy conducts a string quartet and a cast of singers. Giddens' boyfriend and musical collaborator Turrisi is on the small stage, too, thumping on a Sicilian tamburello. They start, stop, start again. The musicians received their parts the day before.

Who am I? Who was I? I had a mother once …

Here, the phrase can be stretched, Kennedy tells the players. Here, articulate more. Here, the violin should counter the viola.

Abels sits up front, listening, making notes. Giddens is on stage, deferential, but also ready to explain this or that. Kennedy is happy to receive her feedback.

And then it comes time for Julie's aria, which Giddens will sing herself, revealing the classical music training she received at the Oberlin Conservatory of Music in Ohio where she studied opera. The corner of her eye catches Kennedy's gestures and signals from the podium. Her voice soars into a lyric soprano's register.

The character is a conceit; she has no basis in Omar's history. Giddens invented her to solve musical and dramatic problems, and to add dimension to a troubling history of racial hostility and abuse.

They sold my daddy down when I was 10. I've never grown as fast as I did then. The last look in his eyes was for me and her. I'll never forget the family we were.

Giddens is taking what she knows about songwriting, and what she knows about classical music and theater, and finding her voice.

"How is it similar to writing a song, and how is it different?" she wonders. A song encapsulates a whole story and typically has a single narrator; an opera tells a story over a longer stretch of time and uses a variety of music expressions, characters and settings.

"This is my choice, my lens, my journey of what he means to me," she says. "We know some things about him, (but) in a lot of ways he's a cipher."

So she makes her choices, as artists do, assigning to Omar an identity and a narrative informed by her own preferences and sensibilities.

This story of Omar, then, is very much also the story of Giddens' discoveries. Although she has devoted her musical career to excavating and celebrating lost and marginalized voices, she knew nothing of Omar ibn Said until the festival asked her to write this opera. She is eager to address her oversight.

* * *

At the spring 2019 workshop, it is time to rehearse the middle passage scene, with its connotations of roiling seas and disorientation. Kennedy asks the musicians for "more bitterness." Abels makes an adjustment to the rhythm in measure 311. Ultimately they all decide to raise the key by a minor third.

The smell, the smell! I cannot stand the smell! Who am I? Who was I? ... I can't remember. I had a mother once.

It is an emotionally taxing portion of an opera taking shape. Later comes the "hoedown," a public celebration replete with double-entendre and smiles meant as sneers.

Our souls are ours to keep.

The segment is inspired by the banjo tune "Old Corn Likker" by Rufus Crisp, which found its way into North Carolina musical lore. African American musician Joe Thompson taught it to Giddens years ago, and she made the song part of an effort to reclaim Black folk music when she was part of the Carolina Chocolate Drops, the Grammy-winning old-time string band whose music is rooted in the Piedmont region of North and South Carolina.

"We're trying to represent ... music that's been erased or forgotten," she says.

This part of the opera emphasizes the cunning of captive laborers who cultivated under duress their double-tongued repartee to satisfy the slavers while signaling discontent to the enslaved. They sing and dance, their words turning ever darker with insinuation once Owen, the slave master, leaves the stage after introducing Omar.

Giddens demonstrates some floor-stomping, addresses the sarcasm barely hidden in the libretto.

She is working through all the scenes, but she's uncertain about a few details, and she hasn't yet settled on the ending. Omar reaches old age in North Carolina, never free, but free enough to hold forth as a respected elder. He has embraced Christianity, though perhaps not relinquished his Muslim faith. He has written his autobiography — a remarkable feat for an enslaved man, evidence of his stature, of his pride, of his unquenchable humanity, and perhaps of an ingrained subversiveness.

Giddens, in search of her ending, is thinking about this.

* * *

Who was I? Who am I?

Giddens is immersed in the history of the transatlantic slave trade, "imagining people from all over Africa, different languages, different religions ... forge community?" She is a wanderer herself, born and raised in Greensboro, N.C., living with her children and her Italian partner near Dublin, accustomed to touring all over the world. She is an embodiment of multiculturalism, and a musical vessel from which pours the artistic concoctions that simultaneously reclaim traditions and invent new ones.

She is a product of the slave trade herself, the flowering shoot grafted onto rootstock as old as the Senegal River.

She is capable of seeing the big picture even as she mines buried cultural veins for the tiniest golden nuggets.

How do you forge community? This is one of the big underlying questions that inform the opera "Omar." But the biggest question, Giddens says, is "Why am I here?" What is the meaning of Omar's fate? What is his purpose in this foreign land, with its foreign ways, its cruelty, its contradictions?

Abels loves this collaboration. He loves contemplating these questions, and finding musical answers. He loves how music can convey ideas and emotions, make references to other cultures, to shared experiences. This is why his scores for the hit movies "Get Out" and "Us" were so successful; they didn't merely heighten the drama or convey a mood — they expressed the story.

Like Giddens, he knew nothing of Omar when first presented with the chance to work on the opera, but Abels knew that mining the past to expose part of the bedrock of American history was exactly what he and Giddens should be doing. And he was delighted at the prospect of working with this famed folk singer who had turned American music inside out.

"She has such a gift for melody," he says. "And people love opera because it communicates so well. ... Rhiannon's process is to get inside a story, to get into history."

They still have work to do together. Some revisions. Some orchestrations. The final scene. They must finish tracking Omar's spiritual journey through time and from place to place. They must finish recovering history.

* * *

This is about Omar's journey — his physical dislocation and accommodations, but also, mostly, his spiritual reconciliations. He grew up

Muslim, studied the Quran, became a leader in his community, then was torn away from all he knew and all he was, only to find himself in a strange place among strange people speaking a strange language and practicing a religion that often was wielded like a weapon.

Giddens wonders: To what extent was his behavior in the American South determined by his faith? To what degree did he manage to retain his rootedness in Islam? Was his apparent embrace of Christianity genuine, or a necessary act of self-preservation in a hostile environment?

And now she must set aside the historical analyses and think about the narrative arc, the story to tell, the drama.

"I'm not writing Omar's story," she clarifies. "I'm writing a version of Omar for the operatic stage. ... At some point you have to leave behind the source material and let the Omar that I'm writing come alive."

And so she is focusing not on his outward struggles: his enslavement, his transport to Charleston, the abuse he endured, his escape to Fayetteville. No, she is looking inward, imagining what Omar might have been thinking: "Why am I here? Why are you doing this to me?"

She is remembering that Omar, and all the other chained Africans shipped to the New World, were not "slaves." They were priests and priestesses, farmers, merchants, artisans, healers, warriors.

"There is no monolithic enslaved person," she says.

They were people whose identities were deleted. But Omar clung to Allah. Omar did not relinquish his past, not completely, not willingly.

Giddens is channeling him. History passes through her and to her pen, to her banjo, to her voice.

"I'm very much a believer that inspiration comes from elsewhere," she says. "The more I'm keyed into that, the more it flows. ... I have to be open as a writer. Some things just come through me."

Don't forget, the character Julie tells Omar. It ain't no shame to hold on tight to memories, to histories ...

The singers stand when it's their turn. At the podium, Kennedy is listening with his ears to the musicians, and with a sort of artistic sonar to the subtle signals Giddens emits — as if he is thinking, "Is this right? Are we on track?"

* * *

It's January 2020, a little more than four months until the opera's premiere, and a new virus is in the air. It emerges in China, jumps to Italy and then the rest of Europe.

By March, the virus is in the U.S., and arts organizations are forced to face a harsh truth: They must cancel their programming. Spoleto Festival USA initially resists, its leaders holding out unfounded hope that the contagion might be arrested sufficiently before late May, but then relents.

Now everything is on hold. "Omar" must wait a year. Giddens is disappointed, but also slightly relieved to have a little more time to work on the opera. Omar was 37 when he was kidnapped in Africa by "infidels," and 61 when, still enslaved in America but able to function with a welcomed degree of autonomy, he wrote his memoir.

During those intervening 24 years, he survived the middle passage, endured for several years the cruelty of his first master in Charleston, managed an escape through forests and across rivers to North Carolina, and ended up the property of a White enslaver, James Owen, who appreciated Omar's religious devotion — though he strived to redirect it toward Jesus.

Owen negotiated his way out of an extortion attempt to keep Omar, and he valued the old Muslim's learning and faith. In a way, the respect was reciprocated.

"I continue in the hands of Jim Owen who does not beat me, nor calls me bad names, nor subjects me to hunger, nakedness, or hard work," Omar writes.

The opera's ending is becoming clearer in Giddens' mind. She is writing it because we have Omar's text, and we have Omar's text because he agreed to tell his story, to satisfy the curiosity of the White people around him who found it difficult to imagine an intelligence and life experience unlike their own.

The ending must affirm his essential humanity — a humanity made possible by will and self-determination, however compromised by the conditions of slavery.

* * *

Giddens maintains a busy schedule despite the pandemic's constraints, finding time to flesh out an aria or rethink a chorus, even as her children compete for her attention.

Then, as if she isn't busy enough, in July 2020 she is named the new artistic director of Silkroad, a multicultural music project started 20 years earlier by cellist Yo-Yo Ma.

In September 2020, Redden announces he will step down as general director the next fall. An international search is on for his replacement. More uncertainty. Redden was a champion of the opera project. Now what will happen? Giddens is anxious.

In November, plans to hold a workshop are set aside due to COVID-related concerns.

* * *

By early 2021, the opera is mostly finished. Though Giddens reserves the right to make changes after on-site rehearsals get underway in April. Then Spoleto announces it will offer a hybrid festival, with fewer events, mask requirements and social distancing. "Omar" will move from the Sottile Theatre to the much larger Gaillard Center, where audiences can be spread out in the hall.

That May, Giddens, Abels, Kennedy, most of the singers and the production team gather in Charleston for run-throughs. It's the first time so many of those involved are together, and the experience is bittersweet.

It reinforces a sense of purpose and solidarity, and reminds everyone of the project's importance, Producer Nicole Taney says.

But this is no way to premier a newly commissioned opera. They will postpone it again. Another year. Another dose of uncertainty. Another potential for scheduling conflicts and the need to recast certain roles.

The delays are difficult to manage. Giddens had been scrambling to convey her music to Abels so he could stitch it all together into a unified whole and create the textures and substance that only a full orchestra can provide, then suddenly she finds herself at home baking biscuits and scones with her kids.

The momentum is disrupted. Giddens' creative muse retreats to a quiet corner and begs for some down time.

At least the premiere likely won't require the festival to accommodate the whims of a dangerous virus and all the compromise that demands. Giddens is quietly relieved, and turns her attention to a recording project with Turrisi — a set of carefully selected and sparsely rendered covers they title, appropriately, "They're Calling Me Home" — that ultimately wins them a Grammy for Best Folk Album.

In July 2021, the festival announces it has chosen scholar and composer Mena Mark Hanna as its next general director. Hanna has Egyptian roots and speaks Arabic. He is a protégé of Daniel Barenboim and Edward Said, who started the the West-Eastern Divan Orchestra, comprised of Israeli and Arab musicians. Hanna has a vested interest in the "Omar" project which is both professional and personal.

When he first applied for the job, he had heard some vague things about the festival's opera commission, he says. By the time Hanna was a finalist, he had learned more.

"It felt like kismet," he says. "It gave me a burning desire to be very forceful in my candidacy for the position. I wanted to be part of the piece."

To present "Omar" in Charleston, where the institution of slavery found its epicenter in North America, where the remnant pain still is felt, is a gift, Hanna says.

"The arts have a way of demonstrating how the past bleeds into the present, and how that gives us a way forward."

And opera, more than other art forms, has a way of fostering an emotional immediacy that's hard to resist, he adds.

"Omar," then, is a kind of emancipation. A historical figure who would have been lost to history but for his autobiography is brought to life. His story finds new expression in the city where he was first enslaved. Omar, finally, is free.

So Hanna is an ally. The accumulation of uncertainty starts to give way, revealing something solid within.

The "upswing," as Giddens puts it, is underway.

* * *

The delays result in one consequential change. Director Charlotte Brathwaite is replaced with Kaneza Schaal.

Brathwaite was essential in helping to conceptualize "Omar" dramatically and aesthetically, Giddens says. But ultimately her vision didn't quite align with what Giddens felt the story demanded.

"I've never written an opera before," Giddens says. "I don't know where the composer stands in the power structure. ... I assumed I had no say."

After all, an opera production is the result of collaboration. Its various elements contributed by people with special talents.

"When you work with other creatives, you want to let them do what they do," Giddens says. "But you have to be on same page."

Clarity comes when Hanna intervenes.

He says to Giddens, bluntly, "It's your opera." Then he suggests Schaal. He is familiar with her work at the Brooklyn Academy of Music and Detroit Opera Theater, and her projects abroad in Rwanda and Egypt. He and the composers love her idea for bringing Omar's text to life onstage.

It's a match.

"At our first meeting, everything that came out of her mouth was stuff that was in my brain," Giddens says.

Schaal has little time to prepare, but she is eager to help stage an important, little-known story, to probe how cultures clash and combine, and to use language itself as a theme: the language of slavery, the language of opera, the language of faith, the language of Omar.

She consults with Giddens and Abels, and quickly assembles her team. She coordinates with Myers, the production designer. They agree that while Giddens' words issue from the mouths of the singers, Omar's words should materialize onstage. The set will be decorated with draped fabric. The clothes worn by the opera's characters will flow with their movement across the stage.

Imprinted or projected on the material will be words and phrases plucked from the autobiography, words and phrases unrestrained by captivity or time.

It's 23 days until opening night and Schaal is in a partitioned section of the Gaillard Center ballroom, rehearsing the last scene of Act 1. Kennedy conducts Renate Rohlfing, who is playing the piano score Abels prepared. Blue tape delineates the dimensions of the stage. Assistants are seated behind a long table taking notes.

Tenor Jamez McCorkle plays Omar who, sleeping, hears his mother's voice.

No matter what they say, I am with you; no matter where you are, I am with you; no matter what they do, I am with you, a part of you.

Johnson, the cruel Charleston slaver played by baritone Malcolm MacKenzie, enters. He is looking for the Muslim man he calls "boy."

Schaal, wearing a head wrap and a one-piece off-white smock that enshrouds her stature and elegance, occasionally rises to consult about stage direction or how a gesture of affection might be rendered.

They get through the scene quickly, and there's time left to run through a portion of an earlier moment in the opera, Julie's escape.

"Let's try it from 298," Schaal says.

The whirlwind has me! Omar sings.

The slave auction has begun, and Omar is sold to the growling Johnson.

At Spoleto Festival's scene shop off the Upper King Street Extension, Director of Production Mike East works closely with Myers and set designer Amy Rubin to build the sets, prepare the video projection and coordinate everything with costume designers April Hickman and Micheline Russell-Brown. His team works from large-format printouts akin to architectural blueprints and uses AutoCAD software to create three-dimensional renderings.

The crew will procure the raw materials to create a flying bridge, rolling staircase, a giant tree made of thick rope, benches and chairs, auction blocks and marketplace walls, some of it draped with printed fabric. "Omar" isn't the only production they are working on. Four others require their labor. The set shop is busy.

* * *

It's nine days until opening night and the orchestra players are assembled for a read-through of the score. Kennedy is on a podium in the Gaillard ballroom offering guidance, encouraging the musicians to use their pencils. Keep the music moving, he says. Quiet down in this passage so we can hear the flute. Play with rhythmic clarity. Emphasize the entrances of each part over the pedal drone.

Abels' contributions become clearer. He has taken Giddens' melodies, her suggestions of harmony and rhythm and style, her storytelling and emotional blueprint, and provided symphonic textures to define mood and pacing to propel the narrative forward. He has transformed tunes into a dynamic whole, into an opera.

A day later, everyone is in the room — the orchestra players, chorus, soloists, both composers, all the crew and assistants — for the first-ever full read-through of "Omar." This is the first time Giddens and Abels hear the work as it was conceived, the first time the singers are accompanied by full orchestra. The anticipation is thick in the air.

It begins with a viola line, then syncopated drumming, an Arabic melody full of augmented seconds. The overture builds slowly, introducing various themes and mixing musical styles. The sadness in the music already is detectable.

Kennedy drives ahead, stopping only once or twice to clarify something. McCorkle is the first human voice we hear. He is in Futa Toro, by the Senegal River, praying.

Praise be to Allah!

Soon his family is threatened by a violent raid, and Omar, along with many others, are cast into the dark and foul hold of a slave ship. Individual choristers sing of their loss — the loss of themselves.

I cannot see, I cannot hear, I cannot feel ...

In the orchestra, the violinists slide their fingers on the strings, downward, suggesting ocean waves.

To the unknown mystery of a land we've never seen, Omar sings.

The orchestra mimics the sound of church bells. The ship has arrived in Charleston.

Take that hat off, boy! the auctioneer commands Omar. And thus a new life of servitude begins. But Omar will continue to look to the east and pray and pray and pray. He will not give up faith in his God. He will not entirely forget who he is.

After more than two hours, at the end of the run-through, the room is silent for a brief moment, then fills with the sound of applause and whistles and bows tapping on the music stands. Kennedy turns to Giddens and Abels. It's rare to have the composers in the room, he says, inviting their feedback.

Giddens tries to respond but stumbles over her words. Abels goes next, and has the same trouble. It takes a moment before they can speak in sentences.

* * *

Three days before opening night, during the first dress rehearsal, McCorkle injures his ankle at the end of Act 1. The pause between acts extends to 45 minutes. When he reappears he's seated downstage right, his left leg, braced, is lifted onto a piano stool. George Johnson, a member of the chorus with his own work to do, is walking the part of Omar as McCorkle sings. The injury concerns everyone, and later the singer is taken to the hospital, which equips him with a stiff protective boot.

The next day, McCorkle has assumed his position stage right, once again seated, as crew readies the Sottile Theatre for another dress rehearsal. Outside, unsettled weather has brought warm, moist air to Charleston. The chance of a late-May thunderstorm is increasing by the hour. It doesn't take long walking in the sun to feel perspiration drip down your back. Inside the venue, the air conditioning is blasting. The seats fill with invited guests, including dozens of students, many wondering whether McCorkle will be sufficiently mobile by opening night.

He sings beautifully, his voice filling the theater with its silvery tone. Johnson, masked, once again is McCorkle's avatar, carefully following Schaal's stage direction, mouthing the words and gesturing as if it were his voice ringing in the Sottile's dome.

The crew is refining its management of the many moving parts, the mechanics of it all. They must hit all the cues: the set-up and take-down of the fabric sets, rope tree, furniture, structures, lighting, video projections. In the pit, Kennedy guides the music-making, working hard to ensure that the opera flows from phrase to phrase, thought to thought, sentiment to sentiment, scene to scene.

The opera takes us from Africa to Charleston, then to Fayetteville. Along the way, Omar questions his fate, yet retains his trust in Allah. Only the One can see the crook in the bend, his mother tells him. It's a turn to us, but it's straight to Him.

His enemies are everywhere. The danger is palpable. But he finds allies, and eventually they urge him to tell his story.

You must, or they will never know and we will fade to dust. Tell your story or they will never know how your battle was won.

* * *

The last dress rehearsal finishes. In two days, Omar's story will come to life on a Charleston stage in the form of the opera written by Giddens and Abels. At least five other opera companies across the U.S. are prepare to mount this production as well — in Los Angeles, San Francisco, Chicago, Boston and Chapel Hill, N.C.

When, 191 years ago, he wrote about his life, Omar addressed the people of North Carolina and South Carolina, but he could not know whether they would ever read his Arabic words, he could not see beyond the crook in the bend. He recorded his story on faith.

But, it turns out, the way was straight, thanks to Rhiannon Giddens and her banjo.

Now the world will know about this Muslim man from Futa Toro near the Senegal River in Africa.

His story is told.

Acknowledgments

L et me be specific: I owe my quick immersion into the work of *The Post and Courier* mainly to three people.

Robert Cox, a writer on the editorial team at the time of my hiring in 2004, who graciously paved the way for an unknown 39-year-old journalist new to the field by arranging for me to apply for an open copy editor position.

Andy Owens, the copy desk manager at the time who knew I wanted to be a writer and who made me promise to pay my dues first, which meant three years on the copy desk, but then cut me loose after just nine months.

Doug Pardue, the special assignments and "Faith & Values" editor at the time who welcomed my contributions while I was still copy editing, and who ushered my work into the pages of the newspaper with enthusiasm — and then edited this book applying his usual instinct, reason and finesse.

All three were important mentors. Bob represented the power of journalism itself. He had been the executive editor of the Buenos Aires Herald during Argentina's Dirty War of the 1970s, and his editorials had saved many lives. He was proof that words have the power to defeat tyrants. Andy personified journalistic integrity and ethics, teaching me the importance of even the smallest blurb in a daily newspaper. Doug was an example of the best kind of editor, one who engages deeply with his staff and who favors a balance of great reporting and great writing.

And so my newspaper career was launched. In the years that followed, I was fortunate to work with some excellent editors and supervisors, and I was privileged to meet a multitude of fascinating people in the Charleston area and beyond. They taught me about the South and its troubled past, how history manifests itself today, how we often fail and sometimes succeed in confronting that past and forging a way forward. They demonstrated the force of faith and community. They revealed the inner workings of the creative mind.

My writing life has been enriched by these encounters, which invariably broadened my view of this complicated place and the fascinating, troubled world beyond. I have been honored to have the opportunity to write stories that address important issues and illuminate the human condition. Thank you to my colleagues who have made this possible, and to the many people — my sources — who have shared their ideas, concerns, fears and joys with me.

CPSIA information can be obtained
at www.ICGtesting.com
Printed in the USA
BVHW091551061022
648774BV00005B/20